FREEPORT MEMORIAL LIBRARY

Presented by

BARBARA HOPKINS

In Memory of

WILFRED L. MORIN

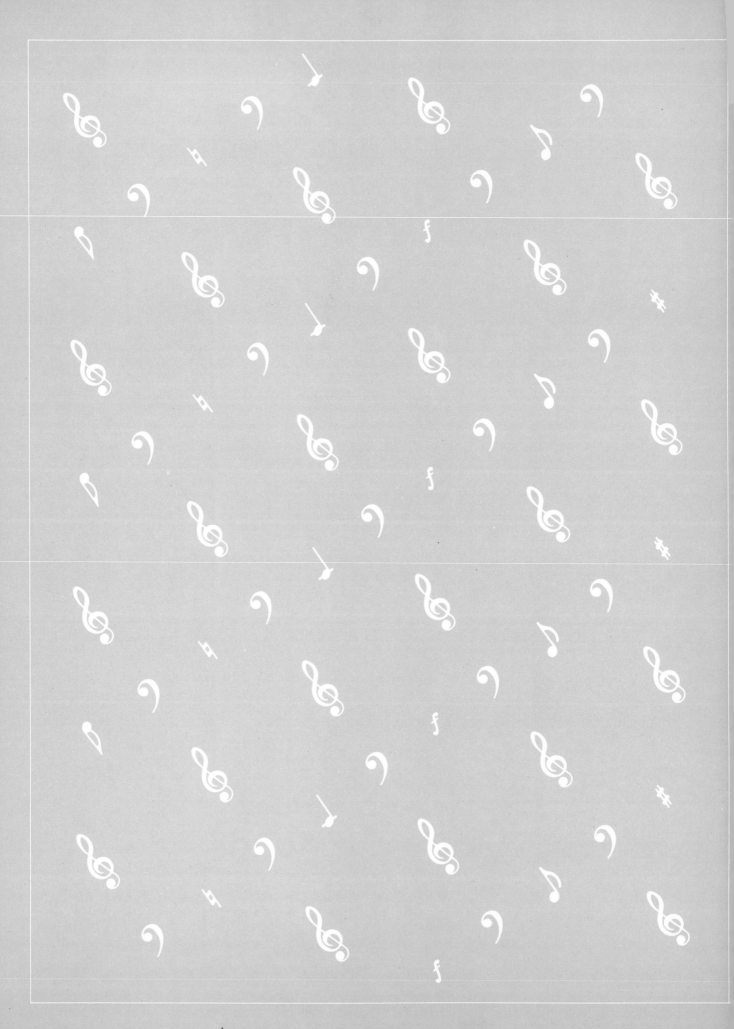

I Hear
AMERICA
SINGING

I Hear
AMERICA
SINGING

A NOSTALGIC TOUR OF POPULAR SHEET MUSIC

LYNN WENZEL & CAROL J. BINKOWSKI

Crown Publishers, Inc.
New York

Frontispiece: Fine coloring and detail enhance the beauty of this rare 1900 Sunday supplement.

Title page: Music was written in honor of many things—even beautiful landscapes, as in this 1852 engraving.

AUTHORS' NOTE: We have tried to be as thorough and accurate as possible in the research, writing, and presentation of this material. Any factual or interpretive errors or omissions are purely unintentional. All statements about particular individuals or groups of individuals are intended only to reflect historical detail as it has been previously stated and are not to be interpreted otherwise. In particular, any references to ethnic or other stereotypes recount only what was actually published in song-sheet form. It is our hope that this will remind all of us that we, as a nation, must continue to advance in understanding and humanity.

A detailed list of permissions begins on page 144.

The illustrations on pages 12–16 courtesy of Foster Hall Collection of the Stephen Foster Memorial, University of Pittsburgh.

Copyright © 1989 by Lynn Wenzel and Carol J. Binkowski

Published by Crown Publishers, Inc., 201 East 50th Street, New York, New York 10022
CROWN is a trademark of Crown Publishers, Inc.

Manufactured in Japan

Library of Congress Cataloging-in-Publication Data

Wenzel, Lynn.
I hear America singing: a nostalgic tour of popular sheet music
Lynn Wenzel & Carol J. Binkowski.
Bibliography
Includes index.
1. Popular music—United States—History and criticism.
I. Binkowski, Carol J.   II. Title.
ML3477.W46   1989
784.5'00973—dc19   88-38393

ISBN 0-517-56967-1

Design by Deborah Kerner

10 9 8 7 6 5 4 3 2 1
First Edition

FOR POPPY,

who gave me the words,

AND SHUMMY,

who gave me the melody.

L. W.

FOR DARIA,

may she always have a song in her heart.

C. J. B.

Contents

"NIGHT AND DAY"
The Thirties

"ALL THE THINGS YOU ARE"
The Forties

"THAT'LL BE THE DAY"
The Fifties and Beyond

"TILL WE MEET AGAIN"

"HOW AM I TO KNOW?"

"CLOSE AS PAGES IN A BOOK"

Foreword

WHY I CHOOSE THE SONGS I SING, how I choose them, is an important thing to me. The songs are my conduits for expressing what I want to say. I do what I do in an effort to touch people and to put *them* in touch with themselves and those around them. We share what we are both feeling at the moment—experience something emotional right now—though it isn't necessarily the same feeling. The songs are my tools and become an extension of me. That's why I choose them so carefully.

Songs can reflect where society is at the moment in the way that the Beatles and Bob Dylan reflected what was going on in the sixties. From the quintessentially American sound of gospel, to Kern's borrowing from the European operetta tradition, to Gershwin's use of the black idiom, our songs reflect the diversity of American culture.

On a personal level, the song that has meant the most to me is Rodgers and Hart's "He Was Too Good to Me." The first moment I heard it sung by Mabel Mercer, it spoke to me of losses that are universal and it said those painful things so simply. I cannot imagine my life without music. I am astonished when peo-ple say music has no part in their lives. It seems to me such a basic human need. I put everything that's important to me—my life, my experience—into my music.

There was a point in my performing life when I began to question all of this: Isn't this a rather shallow way to spend one's life, standing on stage watching people clap their hands together?

But I've come to believe that some do have the gift for touching people and that art is not a frivolous thing. Isaac Bashevis Singer said, in accepting the Nobel Prize, that artists have the ability to put people in touch with everything that is good and noble—and perhaps it will be the artists who save the world.

American popular music joyously connects us with that good and noble strain. *I Hear America Singing* invites us to share in the vitality and grandeur of this heritage.

Barbara Cook

ROBIN RED BREAST

"A crumb of Bread for Robin
His little heart to cheer"

SONG

SUNG BY MADAM ANNA BISHOP

Composed by

J. M. HUBBARD.

NEW YORK
PUBLISHED BY FIRTH, SON & Cº 563 BROADWAY

ROCHESTER   W H DUTTON   A COUSE   J M HUBBARD

"THE PICTURES AND THE SONGS"

Beginnings Through the 1800s

"My Days Have Been So Wondrous Free"

EARLY AMERICAN MUSIC

Some experts say that Indian music, along with European and African, is part of the heritage of American popular music. That seems unlikely, though, as native American music played no historical part in the formation of popular music.

Earliest settlers in Plymouth and Massachusetts Bay remarked on native American music as being lullabies warbled to quiet the children and, somewhere around 1800, a song that purported to be a genuine native American melody was published by George Gilfert in New York and P. A. Van Hagen in Boston. It was "Alknomook, the Death Song of the Cherokee Indians." It had been sung in Mrs. Hatton's *Tammany*, for which James Hewitt had arranged the music (1794), and it became popular in many American drawing rooms.

In reality, native American music is American in a geographical sense only. Beautiful and haunting as it may be, it cannot be thought of as a precursor to

American popular music, but must, nevertheless, be respected for its place in American music history and its thousand-year tradition.

The earliest European music to be heard in North America was French psalmody sung by the Huguenots on the Carolina Coast in 1572, and the English psalmody sung by Sir Francis Drake's seamen in 1579 in California, according to John Tasker Howard.

Freedom to worship was a common goal of many colonial settlers. Such groups dearly enjoyed the privilege of practicing and singing about their faith in a more open atmosphere than they had previously known.

Above: What could be more enticing than the romanticized, imagined luxury of the harem girl's life (c. 1853)?

A beautifully colored and engraved cover, *left,* reflects the Victorian affection for the dwellers of woodland glade and warren (1859). Music such as this which made frequent use of trills and other ornamental motifs was popular with parlor pianists.

This 1856 version of "Yankee Doodle" is one of many editions and renditions of the popular song.

The first recorded use of music on American shores was that of the Pilgrims at Plymouth. The New England colonists enjoyed music that was simple and functional; they were devout and regarded the singing of psalms as an integral part of life. The Pilgrims who sailed from Delftshaven, Holland, in 1620 brought with them the *Book of Psalms*, collected, translated, and published by their pastor in Amsterdam, the Reverend Henry Ainsworth. It integrated the entire Book of Psalms with thirty-nine melodies borrowed from the French, Dutch, and English, and was used by settlers at Ipswich and Salem as well as the Plymouth Colony. It was replaced in 1692 by the *Bay Psalm Book*, whose first published edition probably dates to 1640. The first music book—indeed, the third publication of any kind—in the colonies, the *Bay Psalm Book* was produced by the Massachusetts Bay Colony. It listed 13 melodies for 150 psalms, of which the only tune still familiar to churchgoers is "Old Hundredth." Of course, there was no music in the *Bay Psalm Book* and many congregants could read neither music nor printed English. One can only imagine the cacophonous sound of congregational singing at the turn of the seventeenth century.

This led to the singing school movement, the first American music instruction books, and to singing schools—beginning in 1722. The schools became important not only musically but also socially and were popular meeting places, especially for young men and women of courting age.

The year 1761 marks the date of the next important colonially produced psalter. This was *Urania*, compiled by James Lyon, America's second native composer. The first New England composers appeared in the 1770s, beginning with *The New England Psalm Singer*, or *American Chorister*, engraved in Boston in 1770 by Paul Revere and composed by William Billings. Billings intended to set himself free from the restrictions of earlier hymns and tunes. In all, he published six collections; his church fugues—hymns sung as rounds—remained alive for 150 years among singers in the rural South.

The majority of early music sung in the New World, however, was not written down. Melodies and verses were passed on for generations by word of mouth. They consisted of English, Welsh, Scottish, and Irish tunes that served to strengthen the common bond among families and friends in a strange new land. These tunes—ballads such as "Barbara Allen" and "Sir Patrick Spens"—served as a springboard for the development of American music.

Music breathed its influence into everyday life in colonial America. It bound individuals together to remember their common heritage and faith. It spread news of battles, politics, and other current events. It commemorated heroes, tragedies, and victories. It rallied patriotic spirit and courage when both were sorely needed. Rarely was there a time when music reflected so much of what America was about in such great detail.

As time progressed, melodies remained but new words were added. Songs for every occasion were set to familiar melodies. Many were ballads, or "broadside ballads," which acted as singing newspapers of a sort. Words were printed on sheets or broadsides that were distributed, often hours after a major event, and sung a cappella—without instrumental accompaniment. Since the tunes were known, it was not necessary to publish the music. Copyright laws, as we know them today, did not exist. Therefore, songwriters borrowed freely, and one text might be sung to many familiar melodies and vice versa. "The Death of General Wolfe," one of the first such American broadsides, appeared in 1759.

This form of "songwriting" became increasingly popular as tensions between Britain and the colonies arose. Resistance songs and cries for liberty, in protest against such issues as the Stamp Act, were rampant, and were often sung to such British tunes as "God Save the King." Numerous British and American songs had the same tune. For example, "The British Grenadiers" was also "Free America"; "God Save the King" was also "God Save Great Washington."

The first known published patriotic music appeared in 1768. John Dickinson's "Liberty Song" was set to the British tune of "Hearts of Oak." It urged:

> *Come join hand in hand brave Americans all*
> *And rouse your bold hearts at fair Liberty's call.*

The song was originally published separately—no copy has yet been found—and the words appeared in the *Boston Gazette*. Its popularity spread like wildfire.

Soon the Tory faction issued a parody, which went in part:

> *Come shake your dull Noddles, Ye Pumpkins and*
> *   Bawl,*
> *And own that you're mad at fair Liberty's Call.*

Then parodies of the parody appeared—and so it went. Songs appeared in newspapers, pamphlets, and

THE FAIR ROSE OF KILLARNEY

BALLAD,

by

Miss Eliza Cook,

The Music by

STEPHEN GLOVER.

Baltimore, Published by Geo.Willig Junr.

This ballad was written by the well-known composer Eliza Cook (c. 1836).

broadsides, chronicling growing political dissension and, ultimately, uprising.

"Yankee Doodle" had an illustrious career before, during, and after the Revolution. Although there was no factual basis for the story, the song was said to have been written in 1755 by a certain Dr. Richard Shuckburgh in order to poke fun at the caliber of colonial troops who had gathered to help the British fight the French. Thereafter, the British continued to sing the song in contempt of the colonials.

"Yankee Doodle" was published in 1775 in London with a version about a Yankee coward and his adventures during the French and Indian War. Versions of the song were sung at the Battle of Bunker Hill. However, the Americans soon took the song and tauntingly reversed it on their adversaries. It eventually became associated with the War for Independence as a patriotic song.

Parodies of "Yankee Doodle" abounded. A bawdy one appeared in *The Disappointment*, a spicy "ballad opera." "The Procession, With the Standard of Faction" ridiculed patriots to the familiar tune, and was distributed under the doors of New York households in 1770. "Yankee Doodle" was one of the pieces of

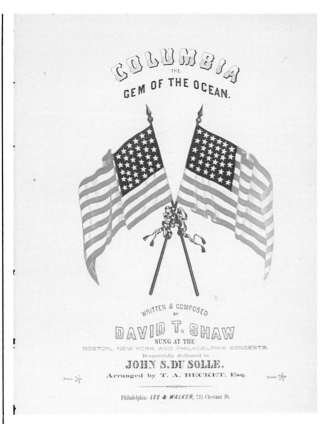

A second edition (1844) depicts the American flag with twenty-six stars and the regulation thirteen stripes. The first edition of 1843 had twenty-five stripes.

Dedicated to Lieutenant Hewitt of the New York Light Guard, this sheet was typical of the many publications of military-inspired music (1840).

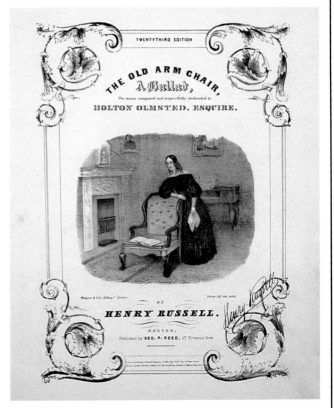

Reflecting the adulation for foreign performers, Signora Pico's "Spanish Song" appeared on an 1845 cover. The engraving is beautifully rendered.

One of the most popular songs by one of the most prolific composers of the early and mid-nineteenth century (1840).

A popular piece for the piano, this sheet music reflects the frequent use of nature for musical inspiration (1860).

American victory music at Saratoga. After Yorktown, it was the tune for many songs that ridiculed the British general Cornwallis.

The well-known Yankee Doodle with "a feather in his cap" was actually seen in print only in the nineteenth century. One of the oldest known American records of "Yankee Doodle" in print was as the "Federal Overture," published by Benjamin Carr in 1794. Music scholars and historians have differed for years over the song's exact publication date or first version, details that will probably never be known exactly.

Songs of the Revolution were turned out in profusion, commemorating battles and events. The Boston Tea Party, the closing of the Port of Boston, the First Continental Congress, war atrocities, enemy failures —all found their way into song.

A rising national consciousness on the part of citizens of the colonies came into view as America ridiculed the British. "An American Parody on the old Song of Rule Britannia" (1774) is an example. A growing force of patriotic spirit was also reflected in song. In 1775, between the battles of Lexington and Bunker Hill, "American Freedom" was popularized throughout colonial America by newspaper. Its stirring words read:

> Hark! 'tis Freedom that calls, come Patriots awake;
> To Arms, my brave Boys, and away;
> 'Tis Honour, 'tis Virtue, 'tis Liberty calls!

Francis Hopkinson, a signer of the Declaration of Independence, was termed America's first composer, having written a comic tune, among others, about outsmarting the British called "The Battle of the Kegs."

The hymn writer William Billings produced the first American musical statement of patriotism. Called "Chester," it was originally written in 1770 with a spiritual text by Dr. Isaac Watts; Billings added patriotic words in 1778. Billings's second "tune book," *The Singing Master's Assistant of 1778*, included "Lamentation Over Boston," about the closing of the Port of Boston. The frontispiece contained an engraving by Paul Revere. "Chester," Billings's best-known tune, remained in use well into the nineteenth century.

The tune of "God Save the King" was used for more and more American songs, including a tribute to George Washington's birthday in 1784. Ultimately, the tune became associated with the familiar "My Country! 'Tis of Thee" in 1831, when Samuel Francis Smith composed the text for a school song.

Washington was the subject of numerous songs, marches, and anthems for his deeds during the Revolution, his inauguration, his presidency, and, ultimately, his death in 1799. "The President's March," believed to have been composed by Philip Phile on the occasion of the 1789 inauguration, became "Hail Columbia" with words by Joseph Hopkinson, and swept the country in 1798. It was first published by Benjamin Carr.

Considered to be the Early National or Federal period (1790–1814), this was a time when songs of politics, war, patriotism, and national figures proliferated. This musical material formed a basis for later songs. "On the Murder of Hamilton," "Madison's March," "Mrs. Madison's Waltz," "President Monroe's Waltz," "John Quincy Adams Grand March," "The National Whig Song," "The Tippecanoe Quick Step," "Brother Soldiers All Hail," "Grand March," "The Acquisition of Louisiana," "Federal March," "Jefferson and Liberty," "Ye Sons of Patriots Gone," "Rise Columbia," "The Ladies Patriotic Song," and "The Siege of Tripoli" were among a few of the titles of the era and beyond.

"Hail to the Chief"—with a tune of British origin from the opera and romance *Lady of the Lake*—was first issued as a three-part chorus in 1812 and later played at President Martin Van Buren's inauguration, gaining rapid appeal thereafter.

Of course, Francis Scott Key's "Star-Spangled Banner" of 1814—set to the British drinking song "Anacreon in Heaven"—moved the country so in its expression of patriotic pride that it became elevated to the status of national anthem.

Secular music began to rise in importance and popularity in the late seventeenth century. Large cities became cultural and intellectual centers of the new land and, as such, cradles for art like their European counterparts.

Many of the first secular songs printed in America were written as airs in ballad and comic opera. New York audiences heard *The Beggars Opera* in 1750 and 1751; *Flora, or Hob in the Well* was performed in Charleston even earlier, in 1735. New York and cities south were operatic centers in America—an antitheater blue law in 1750 in Boston killed opera there for over seven years.

American pleasure gardens, patterned after those in England where concerts, entertainments, and refreshments were enjoyed, were a casualty of the Revolutionary War, but began again with the opening of a new Vauxhall in the 1790s in New York, with music, acrobats, and "illuminations by 500 glass lamps."

The decade from 1795 to 1805 was the peak for the American pleasure garden and the first great period of

American song publication. By 1820, American publishers had issued approximately 15,000 separate works in sheet music as well as more than 500 "songsters," pocket-size collections of song texts.

In the late 1780s and 1790s, a wave of immigrant musicians, mostly from Great Britain, came to America to fill the orchestra pits and stages. Among them were the composers who wrote most of the songs for the thirty years or so after the Revolution.

Benjamin Carr established music publishing houses in Philadelphia and New York, and adapted and arranged stage works for performance. His compositions included the opera *The Archers, or The Mountaineers of Switzerland*, a story of William Tell, as well as some sixty songs, including "Ah How Hapless Is the Maiden" (1800) and "The Little Sailor Boy" (1798).

James Hewitt composed the opera *Tammany, or the Indian Chief*, to a libretto by Ann Julia Hatton (1794), and the popular "The Wounded Hussar" (1800), a dramatic song of war and separation, as well as "The Primrose Girl" (1794), a melodramatic vignette.

Alexander Reinagle was thought to be the best composer in America at the time, and George K. Jackson, organist for the Handel and Haydn Society, wrote cantatas and canons and the secular "One Kind Kiss" (1796), one of the most popular songs in turn-of-the-century America.

From circumstantial evidence it has been determined that America's first native composer was Francis Hopkinson (1737–1791). An intimate friend of George Washington, Hopkinson was the first secretary of the navy and a satirist, poet, lawyer, inventor, and painter. His four secular songs, "The Garland," "Oh Come to Mason Borough's Grove," "With Pleasure I Have Past [*sic*] My Days," and "My Days Have Been So Wondrous Free," lie very much within the style of British pleasure garden and comic opera material. They were never published in Hopkinson's lifetime as there were no true music publishers in the 1760s. Hopkinson was ahead of his time, but unfortunately was not discovered until long after it. There are only a handful of surviving copies as printings were small and none of the copies was printed separately.

Another native-born songwriter was Oliver Shaw. Born in Massachusetts in 1779, he composed "Mary's Tears" and "All Things Bright and Fair Are Thine" —both from poems of Thomas Moore—and his most-popular "There's Nothing True But Heaven." John Hill Hewitt, son of the immigrant songwriter James Hewitt, wrote the very popular "The Minstrel's Return'd from the War," which appeared in 1825 and

Originally written for a musical play in London, this song, *left*, was issued in America in 1812. Its melody later became "Hail to the Chief" and was first adopted as a presidential theme song about 1840. *Right:* The cover is a lithograph of Jenny Lind, the Swedish nightingale, from a daguerreotype. She was the toast of two continents (1848).

remained a favorite for fifty years. His early songs reflected English styles; later ones mirrored the beginning of a national consciousness, an American style that integrated Italian opera, Scottish/Irish melody, and the new minstrel sound. Hewitt's songs included "Wilt Thou Think of Me" (1836), "The Alpine Horn" (1843), "Fall of the Oak" (1841, the answer to Henry Russell's "Woodman Spare That Tree"), and "Ho! For a Rover's Life" (1843). Hewitt continued writing music through the Civil War and eventually composed some three hundred songs.

By the first decades of the nineteenth century, there were hundreds of thousands of Irish immigrants in America. They were known as great singers and music lovers, and a few arrangements of Irish pieces have been found among sheet music published in America in the 1780s and 1790s, songs such as "Coolun" (1798) and "Drimendoo" (1800) and a collection published by James Hewitt in 1807. Irish airs such as "Maggy Lawder," "Derry Down," and "Savourna Deilish" appeared in collections before the turn of the century. The most popular and widely sold collection of Irish songs in America was *Irish Melodies*, with music by Sir John Stevenson and Sir Henry Bishop, respectively, and text by the great Irish poet and musician Thomas Moore. These are among the best-loved songs of the American people and rank in popularity with the songs of Stephen Foster. They were issued in individual sheet-music form as well as in songsters and other music books.

The Irish melodies that have remained beloved and popular to this day include " 'Tis the Last Rose of Summer," with a million and a half copies purport-

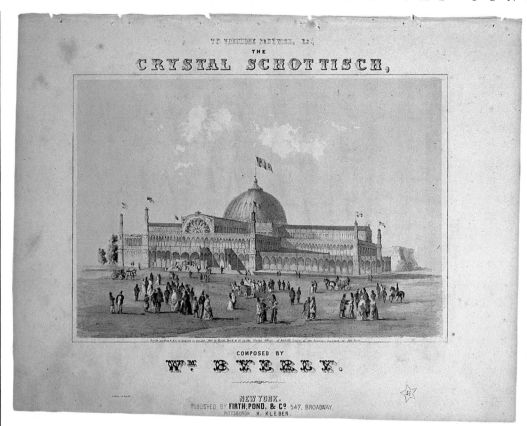

This song sheet commemorates one of the many pleasure gardens so popular in the early nineteenth century (1853).

edly sold in the nineteenth century, "Believe Me If All Those Endearing Young Charms," "The Harp That Once Through Tara's Halls," "Love's Young Dream," and "The Minstrel Boy," sung often today as "Danny Boy." Moore's theme of pensive nostalgia struck an answering chord in America's heart. Seldom have any songs been so widely loved or sung as those of Thomas Moore.

Scottish songs also played an important part in the development of an American musical style. "The Caledonian Laddy," published by Benjamin Carr in 1794, and "Jem of Aberdeen" (1796) were examples of songs written in the Scottish idiom. In 1800, "The Blue Bell of Scotland" appeared. It was one of the

A lovely maiden in a hairstyle popular in 1857 adorns this sepia-toned cover.

most popular songs of 1800–1825 and ranked only behind "Home, Sweet Home" and "Come Rest in This Bosom," by Moore.

Songs by the great Robert Burns began appearing in America in 1800 and included "Comin' thro the Rye," "Auld Lang Syne," and "John Anderson My Jo."

Another important influence on the creation of American music in the late eighteenth and early nineteenth centuries was Italian opera. The music of Mozart, Rossini, Bellini, and Donizetti was widely appreciated. Individual sheet-music editions of songs from operas such as Mozart's *Don Giovanni* and Rossini's *Cinderella* were popular. Bellini's *Norma* premiered in America in 1836; by 1841, it was extraordinarily popular. Boston music publisher Oliver Ditson brought out eight selections, including the best-known "Hear Me, Norma" and "Where Are Now the Hopes I Cherished." Many other titles were published using the music of Bellini set to other lyrics, an example being the song "Katy Darling," to the melody of "Hear Me, Norma." Donizetti's *La Fille du regiment* (*The Daughter of the Regiment*) was also a favorite. Many sheet-music editions were published, some featuring the popular singer Jenny Lind on the cover performing selections from the opera.

Other operas that became immensely popular in America included *The Bohemian Girl* (debut 1844),

An 1856 Sarony lithograph of idealized maidenhood.

Another beautiful nature cover. The engraved peacock's tail is overlaid with hand-applied gold (1850).

Gathering around the parlor piano was a favorite pastime in bygone days. This family group was depicted in 1846.

with its "I Dreamt I Dwelt in Marble Halls" and "Then You'll Remember Me," and Verdi's *Rigoletto*, which had songs created from its favorite melodies such as "Over the Summer Sea" (to "La donna e mobile"). By the middle of the century, however, opera had become musical entertainment for the "aristocracy." Eventually—except for a brief revival during the twentieth century—it would become unheard of to take a melody from an opera and popularize it by affixing new words. Opera and popular music, once one and the same, became two separate genres.

An institution that had a profound effect on the song literature of the eighteenth century was the "singing family." As troupes, these groups traveled countrywide and sang ballads of all types. They often wrote their own music and words and sang in simple harmonies. The best-known was the Hutchinson family from New Hampshire. Others were the Alleghanians, the Cheneys, the Orpheans, and the Harmoneons. In traveling far and wide, these singing families played a large part in creating and spreading the popular songs of the people.

By the late eighteenth century, American dance music found its way into printed music sheets that featured well-known dancers such as Fanny Elssler, often in exotic costume, performing dance numbers. These dances included hornpipes, reels, minuets, the gavotte, the quadrille, and the waltz. Cotillions and country dances were extremely popular in the cities; the music sounded like square-dance music that is thought of today as "country."

The only other purely instrumental music that existed in eighteenth- and early nineteenth-century America were program pieces, especially "battle" numbers. These included sound effects made by cymbals, French horns, cannon, and the like, and were usually episodic, containing various sections with instructions for performance.

The most popular song of the entire nineteenth century was "Home, Sweet Home," composed by Englishman Henry Bishop to a text by American poet John Howard Payne. The tune was written in 1823 as part of the opera *Clari; or, The Maid of Milan*, first performed in London, and six months later in New York at the Park Theatre by a Miss Johnson. It took the country by storm, and it has been claimed that the song sold 100,000 copies during its first year of publication. So many publishers rushed the song into print that it has been impossible to identify the first edition, although it is thought to be one published by George Bacon (Philadelphia, 1823), whose cover reads "sung by Miss M. Tree, in Clari, or The Maid of Milan, At The Theatre Royal Covent Garden." The song was sung by every famous female vocalist, including Jenny Lind and Adelina Patti, and became the favorite of both sides during the Civil War.

The most influential songwriter in America during the first half of the nineteenth century was Henry Russell (1817–1900). Born in Britain, he came to America in the 1830s as a church organist and soon became a professor of music at the Rochester Academy of Music in New York. His first printed song, "Wind of the Winter's Night, Whence Comest Thou?" (1836, words by Charles MacKay), was borrowed from Italian opera style, and started him off on a career as vocalist, keyboardist, and songwriter. The songs he was to write were simple pieces, suitable for the eager parlor amateur, and, as a group, sold more sheet music than any others before Stephen Foster. "The Old Arm Chair," perhaps the most popular (1840), with a text by Eliza Cook, was a sentimental ballad designed to wring the last drop of emotion from the listener. It went, in part:

I've treasured it long as a holy prize,
I've bedewed it with tears, and embalmed it with sighs;

Would you learn the spell—a mother sat there,
And a sacred thing is that old armchair.

Also popular was "Woodman, Spare That Tree" (words by newspaperman George P. Morris, 1837), a story about a woodcutter who refrains from chopping down a tree that sheltered him when he was a boy. It remained in print until well into the twentieth century. Russell's songs reflect the concerns of the nineteenth century—longing for youth, home, old friends, and more innocent times—themes that wind like a leitmotiv through much popular music of the day. A good businessman, Russell understood that although he had been trained in the classics, opera, and sacred music, the audience in America for classical music was diminishing while that for popular music was growing at a phenomenal rate.

During the first half of the nineteenth century, indeed, the business of music had begun to develop. Musicians could make real money from their skills. Mass-production methods enabled sheet music to become available to larger populations, and the practices of promotion and advertising became more sophisticated. Music historian Gilbert Chase postulates that by the middle of the nineteenth century the conditions necessary for regular consumption of, and interest in, art were in existence. Large populations had been established, wealth was being accumulated, and leisure time was considered not only acceptable but desirable. Music, as an art form, could now become a major economic enterprise.

Music as an art, however, was something else entirely. With the exception of that of Stephen Foster, much popular music of the late eighteenth through the early nineteenth century was far from artistic. Most songs suffered from a mawkish sentimentality which today can evoke laughter. What seems ridiculous to us now, however, answered the needs of people who were as yet aesthetically immature. If a piece were to succeed, it had to be blatantly emotional rather than subtly moving. Traveling virtuosi, few of them Americans, relied on the most outlandish exhibitionism to obtain patrons—and they were very successful. The hardest-working, struggling wage earner would willingly plunk down a good percentage of his pay to see a renowned singer or violinist in concert, sit in frozen rapture throughout the performance, and partake afterward in the casting of adulation upon the performer's head. One might say this was the beginning in America of the "star" system.

The split that had begun to occur in the early 1800s between classical and vernacular music was all but completed by midcentury. The frontier had opened up and families were heading west in ever greater numbers. The men, disdaining the old concepts of leisure, were interested in land and money and conquest. Time spent in genteel pursuits must have seemed wasteful to the gnarled pioneer with dreams of gold. So, gradually, popular music, with its emphasis on sentiment, home, mother, gentle pursuits, and loss of love and innocence, became the province of women. A skill at the piano, the creation of the parlor musicale, and the resultant safe haven of home against the evils "outside" became one of the attributes of the cult of domesticity and its complete separation of male and female spheres that reached its zenith in the late nineteenth century. All this was reflected in America's sheet music.

"Willie, My Brave"

THE MUSIC OF STEPHEN FOSTER

SING "OH, I COME FROM ALABAMA wid a banjo on my knee," "I dream of Jeanie with the light brown hair," or "Way down upon the Swanee River," and any listener will shout, "Stephen Foster!"

Many people do not realize, however, that the breadth of Foster's work reached far beyond the confines of these familiar tunes. He penned songs of war such as "Was My Brother in the Battle?" ("Tell me, tell me weary soldier from the rude and stirring wars/ Was my brother in the battle where you gained those noble scars?"). He wrote sad and sentimental songs such as "Gentle Annie" ("Thou wilt come no more, gentle Annie/Like a flower thy spirit did depart"). And, of course, there were plantation songs in dialect such as "Old Black Joe" and "Camptown Races" ("De long tail filly and de big black hoss, Doodah! doodah!").

One of America's most beloved nineteenth-century

One of Stephen Foster's lesser-known "Willie" songs (1851).

Typical of publishers' practices of the time, the composer's autograph on the sheet-music cover was printed, not handwritten (first edition, 1854).

composers, Foster left a prolific song legacy—more than two hundred compositions—that hallmarked the country's rapid sociopolitical expansion and up-heaval during the mid-1800s.

Foster was one of the greatest melodists America has ever produced. His writing tapped veins of emotion and beauty that, until that time, American popular song had not seen. His seemingly simple writing manner, folk in style, without ornamentation or elaboration, caused his music to rise above most of the rest.

Foster's music grew out of both the middle-class fondness for sedate and sentimental music of the time and the stirring black spiritual sounds that impressed him deeply as a youth. It also reflected both his own and America's pain and fall from innocence experienced with the approach of the Civil War. As Foster perpetuated traditional music concepts, enhanced them, and then set a new style, so too the country moved from old tradition to strike new patterns in terms of politics and human rights. His sensitivity to the fabric of American culture, as well as to the joys and sorrows of individuals, make him the source of some of our true American folk songs.

Stephen Collins Foster was born on Independence Day in 1826, the youngest in a respectable middle-class family in Lawrenceville, Pennsylvania. His talent and interest in music were apparent early, but polite society and family tradition frowned upon music as an occupation. It and related cultural arts were considered pursuits to be followed by the "gentler female sex" in order to provide them with an aura of polish and refinement. However, Foster's family loved their unusual child and indulged his interests as best they could, while constantly worrying about his health and his ability to cope with the future. They seemed pleasantly amazed by the songs he produced in his teens, such as "Open Thy Lattice, Love" and "The Tioga Waltz." Yet they would have been more comfortable if he had chosen the path of business instead.

Young Stephen absorbed as much music as possible, from the parlor songs performed at family gatherings to the Negro spirituals sung at church services he attended with a favorite servant, Lieve. Stephen was particularly fascinated by the latter category, and it left a deep impression on him that was reinforced by his observance of black workers in Pennsylvania and their stirring songs.

Foster's first published song, "Open Thy Lattice, Love," appeared in 1844. Its musical style is that of a true art song with the flow of a barcarole, and may be traced to stage and concert songs of English writers. The words, by George P. Morris, had been printed in the October 14, 1843, issue of *The New Mirror;* Foster most likely read them in the magazine. He was eighteen, and his song was dedicated to Susan Pentland, a lifelong friend. The song had two printings by George Willig of Philadelphia; the first edition contains an error—Foster's name is given as L. C. Foster.

He produced a fine variety of "Ethiopian" songs—those with strong rhythms, often comic dialect, and simple but memorable melodies. "Oh! Susanna" is a prime example. Entered in a contest sponsored by the Eagle Ice Cream Saloon in Pittsburgh, it gained rapid popularity—so rapid, in fact, that the musical director of the saloon tried to steal the song the day after the contest, even though it was not awarded first prize.

That song, along with "Lou'siana Belle" and "Old Uncle Ned," was written for a young men's club that met twice a week at Foster's home. The agenda consisted of amateur theatricals and singing, using such early minstrel songs as "Jump Jim Crow" and "Coal Black Rose." Success at the club, carried by members' word of mouth to other parlors and from there to the concert stage, spread the songs' reputation quickly. They were heard by W. C. Peters, who asked for copies for publication. Foster readily agreed. He received no payment at all for "Lou'siana Belle" or "Old

Uncle Ned." "Oh! Susanna" brought him an outright payment of $100. Typical of the day, publishers and performers were the big money-makers, with their names often prominently featured on the sheet-music covers. The composer received short shrift, both in money and in notoriety.

These songs betrayed the influence the minstrel shows had had on Foster's musical thinking and were his first truly successful pieces, the ones that established his fame in America and abroad, and the first written in a style that was distinctly his own.

Daguerreotype of Stephen Foster, June 12, 1859, at age thirty-two, taken in a shop on Wood Street, Pittsburgh, next door to his music studio.

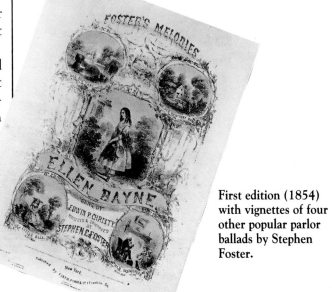

First edition (1854) with vignettes of four other popular parlor ballads by Stephen Foster.

A first edition (1854) of Foster's song about his wife, Jane, whom he called Jennie.

The growing propaganda for abolition of slavery had inspired sentimentality toward an oppressed people. That this Northern reaction found its voice in the songs of Stephen Foster was paradoxical. Foster was the son of slave-owning Democrats who strongly opposed abolition. But whatever its genesis, Foster's exposure to the minstrel show played a significant part in what he believed to be authentic depictions of black American life and character.

The core of the minstrel repertory during the 1840s and 1850s was the "plantation song," with its gentle, sympathetic treatment of black characters. After "Old Uncle Ned" (1848), which treated blacks in a traditionally offensive manner, Foster's music reflected a more sympathetic view.

Within a year of its publication, "Oh! Susanna" became the marching song of the "forty-niners" on their way to California during the gold rush, and was always thereafter connected with the pioneers. It was also reportedly heard in some astonishingly remote places, such as India and North Africa, as well as in Germany, France, and Sweden. "Oh! Susanna" truly became a worldwide hit. W. C. Peters, Foster's publisher, is said to have made $10,000 from the song. Early editions are prized by collectors, and a pirated edition issued by C. Holt, Jr., of New York ten months before the Peters one, copyrighted February 25, 1848, is a rare treasure. Only three copies of the first edition are known to be in existence. The success of "Oh! Susanna" decided Foster on his permanent career. From then on, he practiced nothing but songwriting.

Even though Foster enjoyed composing "Ethio-

pian" songs, he felt ambivalent about signing his name to them. Today, he would not have to be apologetic for his preferences, but in pre–Civil War times, open acceptance was withheld. If one were to compose at all, it was only respectable to produce "genteel" music for parlor or recital gatherings. Foster tried hard in this vein too, perhaps because he felt that it would compensate for his family's disappointment when he shunned a career in business by giving up bookkeeping and turned to songwriting full time.

"Oh! Susanna" was Foster's first song to be associated with the Christy Minstrels. Their success with several of his songs on the concert stage prompted Firth, Pond & Company in New York—a leading publisher which was to print a major portion of Foster's songs until his death—to bring out four of his minstrel tunes in 1850. These were "Nelly Was a Lady," "My Brudder Gum," "Dolcy Jones," and "Nelly Bly." Again, his remuneration was often small for these publications. "Nelly Was a Lady" gained him only a payment of fifty free copies from the publisher.

Also published by Foster in 1850 were "Oh! Lemuel," "Dolly Day," "Gwine to Run All Night" ("Camptown Races"), and "Angelina Baker." With the exception of "Oh! Lemuel," these songs were called plantation melodies, and differed from early minstrel songs in their transformation of black Americans from simple, amusing, and illiterate creatures to gentle, kindly, and profoundly human beings, an important step in the consciousness-raising process that would eventually bring Americans to regard slavery as sinful.

Other works from 1850 are "Molly! Do You Love Me?" "Lily Ray," and "Way Down in Cairo." Foster experimented with two instrumental numbers, the "Soirée Polka" and "Village Bells Polka." He also published what are referred to as his sentimental songs: "Ah! May the Red Rose Live Alway," "The Voice of By Gone Days," "The Spirit of My Song," "Turn Not Away," and "I Would Not Die in Spring Time" (written under the name of Milton Moore). Foster had been raised in a well-to-do family where art and culture were cultivated and had been exposed early to eighteenth-century ballad styles. In "Ah! May the Red Rose" particularly can be felt the influence of English and Irish melodies. Yet the lovely lyricism of that and others did not enjoy much vogue during Foster's lifetime. Their day had passed, replaced in popularity by the minstrel song and Italian opera—which style also influenced Foster, notably in "Wilt Thou Be Gone Love" and "Beautiful Dreamer."

In 1850, Foster married Jane McDowell, a doctor's

daughter. Their marriage was difficult from the first and ended in separation and unhappiness for both. Foster was childish and had been indulged and spoiled by his mother and siblings. Jane did not share his interest in music and resented Foster's inability to support them as well as, later, his drinking. She nagged. He withdrew. Later, when his drinking became uncontrollable, she left for good. In spite of all this, evidence exists of their love for each other. We know it from Foster's point of view from the beautiful and tender "Jeanie with the Light Brown Hair," written for his wife after one of their separations in 1854 ("Jeanie" being a form of her nickname, "Jennie"). "Old Black Joe" was written with an old servant of Jane's family in mind, remembered from happier days.

One of Foster's most famous songs, "Old Folks at Home," featured E. P. Christy's name on the cover. Christy, one of the leading minstrel performers of the day, was a shrewd man. Foster initially assigned to him not only the performing rights, but also the privilege of being listed as the composer, as he did not want to be known for his "Ethiopian" songs. Christy paid for use of "Old Folks"—a controversy exists as to whether it was $15 or $500—and agreed to omit Foster's name. The first cover was issued by Firth, Pond & Company, and the title page described it as an "Ethiopian Melody . . . sung by the Christy Minstrels, written and composed by E. P. Christy." By 1852, the song had sold 40,000 copies, making it one of the highest sellers of all time. Foster now developed second thoughts about passing off these songs as the work of others, and in 1852 he wrote to Christy asking that he be publicly credited as the author on all future editions. Christy refused to change the agreement on "Old Folks" despite Foster's vow to devote himself "openly and without shame" to "Ethiopian" music. Christy's name appeared as composer in elaborate lettering until the copyright was renewed. After 1852, the songs Foster wrote for Christy bore Foster's name, but he still charged Christy little more than a pittance for performing rights.

In 1851, Foster brought out "Melinda May," "Sweetly She Sleeps, My Alice Fair," "Once I Loved Thee, Mary Dear," "Laura Lee," "Eulalie" (with H. S. Cornwall), "Farewell My Lillie Dear," "Willie, My Brave," "I Would Not Die in Summer Time," "Wilt Thou Be Gone Love?" "Farewell Old Cottage," "My Hopes Have Departed Forever," "Ring de Banjo," "Oh! Boys, Carry Me 'Long," and "Give the Stranger Happy Cheer." But most important of that year, or any other, Foster produced "Old Folks at Home." It was and remains a classic of the simple folk style and shares with "My Old Kentucky Home" the

honor of being the most played and sung of all the Foster songs and also one of the most popular in the world.

What are considered by some to represent Foster at his inspirational peak, certainly in the plantation genre, are five songs written between 1851 and 1853. They are—in addition to "Old Folks at Home," "My Old Kentucky Home," and "Farewell, My Lillie Dear"—"Massa's in de Cold Ground" (1852) and "Old Dog Tray" (1853). These songs have less to do with ethnicity and more with nostalgia, and were written at a time when Foster faced severe personal problems: the separation from his wife and the realization that home and family, as he wistfully and sentimentally saw them, were never to be his. This group represents the coming to an end of Foster's career as a writer of minstrel songs. He wrote only a handful more during the last ten years of his life, and none matched the melodic greatness of those earlier songs.

In 1854, Foster wrote three "good" songs, two of somewhat lasting fame, "Ellen Bayne" and "Willie, We Have Missed You," and the third, the lovely, lyrical "Jeanie with the Light Brown Hair." When "Jeanie" was first published it was moderately successful and earned Foster $217.80 in its first two and a half years. Then, needing cash, Foster sold his future rights to it and a number of other songs. After his death, the renewals reverted to his wife and daughter, but the song brought them very little. In 1891, the publishers paid Jane and Marion Foster seventy-five cents, the royalties due on three cents a copy.

After "Jeanie," Foster fell into a slump. It is hard not to believe that domestic and financial problems weighed so heavily on him as to dry up inspiration. In any case, for five years he produced only mediocre work, with the possible exception of "Hard Times Come Again No More" (1855) and the definite exception of "Come Where My Love Lies Dreaming" (1855). The latter is one of Foster's most ambitious songs and, some say, one of his best. There is a distinctly Schubertian quality and a strongly felt consciousness of Italian operatic melody in this art song written five months after the death of Foster's mother and less than a month before that of his father.

"Gentle Annie" (1856) was a good but not a great song, and Foster's dry period continued until 1860. In that year, Foster produced "Old Black Joe" which ends the cycle of sympathetic black character studies, and ranks among Foster's top ten works—deceptively simple and melodically evocative.

By the time "Old Black Joe" was written, Foster's marriage was as good as dead. Alone, he had moved to New York City with a guarantee of income if he

Broadsides ("penny sheets") of two songs by Stephen Foster distributed during the Civil War, "Beautiful Dreamer" and the war song "Bring My Brother Back to Me."

could deliver a certain number of songs each year. He had sold out his interest in the remaining established hits of previous years in order to keep up with a constant overdrawing of bank accounts. For a while, he worked steadily and remained relatively sober.

As the country progressed from sedate innocence to trying times, so did Foster. His increasingly serious social/personal concerns paralleled the country's inexorable march toward the terrible realities of the Civil War. Attempting to use the war as an inspiration, Foster wrote prolifically in 1861, 1862, and 1863, but none of his efforts was worth remembering, with the possible exception of "We Are Coming, Father Abraam" (words by Jas. Sloan Gibbons), inspired by President Abraham Lincoln's plea for 300,000 more volunteers.

In the last full year of Foster's life, 1863, he published forty-six new songs, but their quality, sadly, showed all too clearly his disintegration into an alcoholic haze and the destruction of the tubercular man's once great talent.

Foster's genius sparked once more in "Beautiful Dreamer," popularly supposed to have been the last song he wrote. It was actually written two years before his death, but not brought out until 1864 by Firth, Pond & Company to capitalize on the composer's tragic demise.

Stephen Collins Foster died as a direct result of a fall in his miserable hotel room in the Bowery. He had gashed open his throat, bruised his forehead, and burned himself by overturning a container of boiling water. Foster was found naked and suffering on the floor by a friend and collaborator, George Cooper. He lingered a short while at Bellevue Hospital and died, most probably of the combined effects of tuberculosis, alcoholic deterioration, and malnutrition. Quite literally, in despair, depression, and frustration, Foster self-destructed. He was thirty-seven.

The tragedy of Foster's life is that he dissipated his enormous talent as recklessly as he did his energy and his financial future. He was ingenuous, impractical, and incapable of adjusting to the realities of life. His dreams and fancies to which he withdrew made him unable to care for himself properly, and his final years were a sad mixture of drunkenness, poverty, self-pity, depression, and loneliness. Thirty-eight cents and the clothes on his back were what he owned when he died.

But what he left the world—at least a dozen songs unmatched in the annals of American popular music—for that no payment would have sufficed. His final words, scrawled on a piece of paper found in his pocket, were "Dear Friends and Gentle Hearts."

"Coal Black Rose"

MINSTREL SONGS

AMERICA HAS ALWAYS BEEN FASCINATED with the customs of its black population, particularly the musical ones. Their spiritual songs, unique rhythms, characteristic dialect, instrumental combinations, and even gestures and movements easily influenced popularly staged entertainments from colonial times to the present. The rise of the minstrel show and song, offering commentary on as well as parodies of black life and music, held the public's rapt attention for decades during the 1800s.

Black music was rooted in the varied African rhythms of the slaves. A life of toil and bondage added a plaintive mood to melodies and words, and the promise of release from misery offered by Christianity served to further deepen and enrich the musical expression. Spirituals that were both somber and

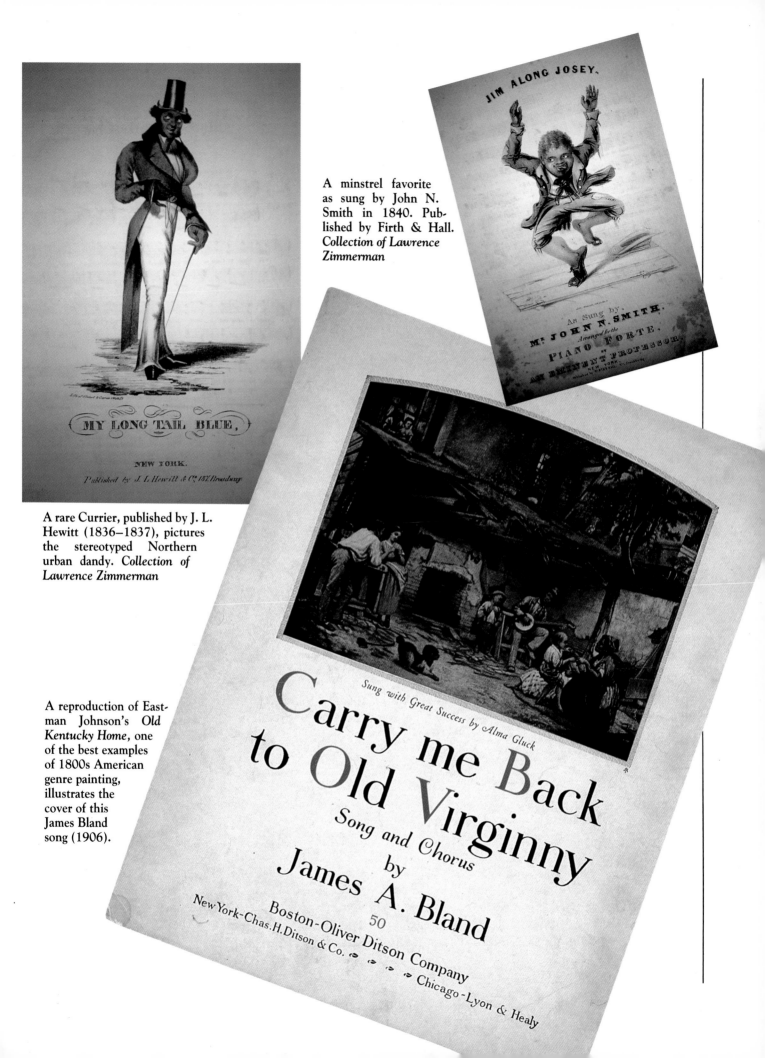

A rare Currier, published by J. L. Hewitt (1836–1837), pictures the stereotyped Northern urban dandy. *Collection of Lawrence Zimmerman*

A minstrel favorite as sung by John N. Smith in 1840. Published by Firth & Hall. *Collection of Lawrence Zimmerman*

A reproduction of Eastman Johnson's *Old Kentucky Home*, one of the best examples of 1800s American genre painting, illustrates the cover of this James Bland song (1906).

"Young Folks from Home," *left,* is called the companion piece to Foster's "Old Folks at Home" and was written by H. Craven Griffiths in 1853.

Right: One of the Christy Minstrels' popular songs, "Way Down South in Alabama."

exuberant developed, intended to be sung chorally, individually, or in a call-response mode. Other black songs proliferated as well—labor songs, songs of life-long sorrow, and nonsense songs. Such material was contained in the vast heritage of black music and laid the partial groundwork for minstrelsy, with its mirrors and distortions of the black character.

As early as 1769, there was a record of a performance done in "blackface" (a white performer rubbing burnt cork onto his face), and in 1799 "The Gay Negro Boy" was performed by Gottlieb Graupner. The 1796 song "I Sold a Guiltless Negro Boy" reflects this era's sometimes sympathetic and sentimental portrayal of blacks.

Fascination with the lives and plight of blacks grew and more songs containing dialect—known as Ethiopian melodies—were written. As Americans celebrated their lives with sentimental tunes of love and loss and created oases of refinement by re-creating German and Italian opera in their parlors, another kind of vernacular music began to flourish among the masses—the minstrel show.

Minstrelsy was really British in its ancestry, as was much late eighteenth- and early nineteenth-century music. It had not been uncommon for British theater to include Negro characters and "Negro songs," usually sentimental and patronizing. British comedians blackened their faces and performed their interpretations of Negro behavior.

American interpretations of British minstrelsy as

well as of black stage entertainment in the 1820s and 1830s tended, finally, to settle into two stereotypes that endured throughout the half-century-long popularity of the minstrel show. One was the ragged plantation hand, poor but happy; the other was the Northern urban dandy in fashionable clothes, silk hat, and walking cane, who aped exaggerated white behavior.

Before long, blackface comedians gathered into troupes and enlarged their repertory of skits, dances, and songs. Dark swallowtail coats, white pantaloons, and striped calico shirts punctuated their appearance. They sang songs such as "The Essence of Old Virginia" and "The Lucy Walk Around," occasionally exchanging comic banter. Audiences clamored for more.

Other troupes quickly followed and came to include the Christy Minstrels, Bryant's Minstrels, the Sable Harmonists, and the Ethiopian Serenaders, among others. These groups traveled across America singing solo songs in dialect, intoning satirical dialogues, performing burlesque, and otherwise entertaining with instrumental pieces and dances as well as "walk arounds."

The minstrels culled their musical material from many sources: folk music, British music hall material, Italian opera, Scottish-Irish folk tunes, Negro spirituals, early plantation music, white revival music, and Western and Southern working songs. Eventually these bands created a music of their own, truly American and original in its style and performance.

The popularity of minstrelsy spread far and wide quickly, often much to the dismay of the purveyors of the "genteel" tradition, although in truth, this music was more truly evocative than the overly sentimental mush of the drawing room. The lively, inventive music had reached California by the late 1840s, and eventually popped up all over the world. Even Britain's Queen Victoria was entertained by an American minstrel band.

"The Bonja Song" (1820), "Massa Georgee Washington and General Lafayette" (1824), and "Coal Black Rose" (1827) were among early minstrel works. The banjo, fiddle, bones, tambourine, the triangle, and the struck jawbone of an ass, ox, or horse (whose teeth rattled when hit) were all instruments used by the bands.

Early blackface entertainers included George Washington Dixon, George Nichols, Bob Farrell, and "Jim Crow" Rice. Nichols claimed authorship of the song "Zip Coon" (to the familiar tune of "Turkey in the Straw"), which personified the urban dandy character, but so did Dixon and Farrell. It was left to Rice, however, to popularize it. G. W. Dixon was doing Negro songs in blackface in 1827, and in 1829 he appeared in New York, where he introduced one of the most favored numbers in his repertoire, "Coal Black Rose." A sheet-music edition published by Firth and Hall goes "Lubly Rosa Sambo cum,/Don't you hear de Banjo tum, tum, tum," and the cover includes a sketch of "Lubly Rosa" and "Sambo" playing on the African gourd banjo known as the "bonja" or "banja." The banjo as we know it developed from a primitive four-string gourd to the modern five-string instrument by 1845.

Dixon also claimed the authorship of "Long Tail Blue," which he featured in his performances from 1827 on.

"Daddy" or "Jim Crow" Rice's real name was Thomas Dartmouth Rice. Often referred to as the father of American minstrelsy, he was a New Yorker who began his stage career as an itinerant player. After seeing a poor, old, somewhat bedraggled Negro man oddly limping and singing a strange song, he quickly formed an imitation and, in 1828, interpolated it between the acts of a play, as was done in all the theaters. The subsequently famous stage routine consisted of Rice in blackface doing a series of odd movements and jumping at the appropriate time. His song (1828) was called "Jim Crow." Its refrain went:

Wheel about and turn about,
And do jis so;
Ef'ry time I wheel about,
I jump Jim Crow.

A number of different sheet-music editions were published, most featuring lithographs of "Daddy Rice" gotten up as the stage stereotype of the black dandy. The song made Rice famous and became a huge international hit. Rice was also the creator of many farces and burlesques known as Ethiopian operas, blackface extravaganzas that included many "plantation" melodies. These shows were the forerunners of the variety acts that were incorporated into the second half of the minstrel show after it became formalized. A forerunner of musical comedy, it consisted of spoken dialogue, songs, and dances loosely knit together. Thomas Rice wrote several of them, including "O Hush, or The Virginny Cupids," "Long Island Juba," and "Bone Squash." Lavish productions such as these lacked the spontaneous imagination of the earlier shows.

Rice is mainly associated with this early period. The other composer and performer associated with the early period was E. P. Christy, whose Christy Minstrels interpreted and performed minstrel shows for more than fifteen years. It was Christy who structured the minstrel show format into its more refined state. He combined variety entertainment ("olio"), a Mr. Tambo and Mr. Bones routine ("end men" responding with gags to questions by Mr. Interlocutor), and a burlesque of free-form entertainment performed earlier in the show. His group presented 2,500 performances in New York alone in addition to touring. Other groups such as the New York Minstrels and the Ethiopian Minstrels copied his style and format.

The most prominent minstrel song composers of the 1840s to the 1860s were Stephen Foster and Dan Emmett. Foster wrote plaintive plantation melodies for the first half of the show—for example, "Uncle Ned"—while Emmett composed humorous "walk arounds" for the plantation festival portion performed by the whole company at the show's end. "Dixie" is the most widely known and long-lived number by Emmett, but he also wrote some of the most popular songs of the 1840s, 1850s, and 1860s, including "Old Dan Tucker," "T'will Nebber Do to Gib It Up So, I'm Gwine Ober de Mountains," "Blue Tail Fly," "Root, Hog or Die," and "Jordan Is a Hard Road to Trabel." In 1858, Emmett joined Bryant's Minstrels, the finest group of the time, for whom he wrote his best songs, including "Dixie."

Although Southerners would like to claim "Dixie" as their own, Daniel Decatur Emmett's name on the original edition by Firth, Pond & Company in 1860 clearly indicates his authorship of the great popular song. Emmett wrote both words and melody; the tune owes something to Scottish-Irish folk melodies, but is still quite original. The words have their source in earlier minstrel styles of the 1840s—lines such as "I wish I was in . . ." and "Away down South" appeared often in other minstrel songs. It was, after all, the custom of minstrels to borrow from one another. Performed first in 1859, the song spread like wildfire. From 1860 on, publishers in the North and South issued it in many forms, much of the time giving no credit to Emmett. The list of editions is long, and Emmett realized very little money from it. The tune was used by both the Northern and Southern sides of the Civil War, but its status remained as a Confederate symbol. Eventually it became representative of all that was truly American—an optimistic jauntiness and cockiness of spirit which, even after the devastation of the war, reasserted itself in rebuilding shattered lives and pioneering Western frontiers.

Other favorite minstrel songs included "Jim Along Josey" (1838), "Clare de Kitchen" (1830s), and

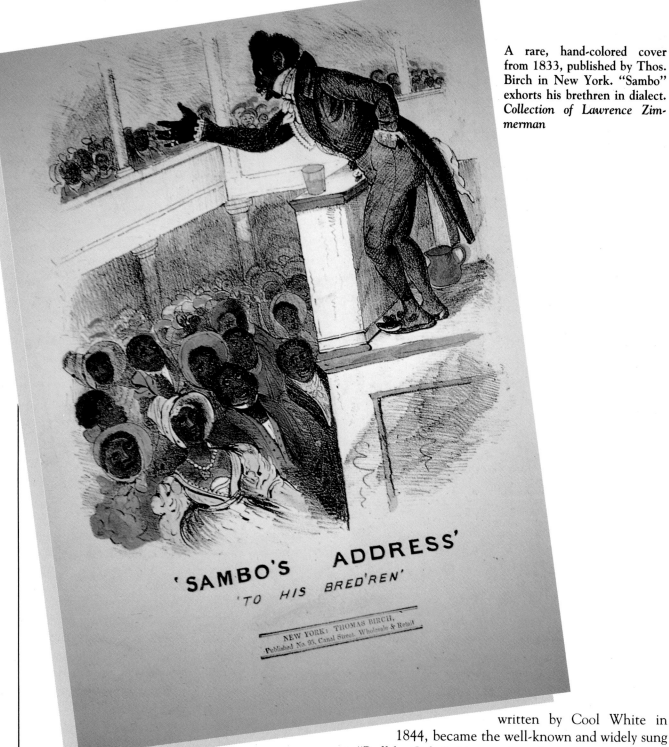

'SAMBO'S ADDRESS'

'TO HIS BRED'REN'

NEW YORK: THOMAS BIRCH,
Published No. 95, Canal Street, Wholesale & Retail

A rare, hand-colored cover from 1833, published by Thos. Birch in New York. "Sambo" exhorts his brethren in dialect. *Collection of Lawrence Zimmerman*

"Long Time Ago," whose words and music—"Oh I was born down ole Var-gin-ee/ Long time ago./ O Massa die an make me fre-e/ Long time ago"—were probably originally a variation of a plantation song sung by slaves. Its words went, "As I was gwoin down Shinbone Alley;/Long time ago!/ To buy a bonnet for Mis Sally/ Long time ago!" Syllabification of words for rhythmic purposes was one of the stylistic antecedents that would enable Elvis Presley to find the voice of rock-and-roll.

"Lubly Fan (Will You Come Out To Night?),"

written by Cool White in 1844, became the well-known and widely sung "Buffalo Gals." Many minstrel songs are still sung today in the backwoods, songs we think of now as folk tunes. They are distinctly American and include "Old Gray Goose," "Jonny Boker," and "I'm Gwine Ober de Mountains."

Although the songs were borrowed from eighteenth-century opera buffa, plantation styles, and black dialects, among others, they became truly the most American work yet known, assimilating the essence of the growing nation. The banjo became a focal point of the shows and was featured in complex arrangements requiring a fair degree of virtuosity. The bands as well as banjo and fiddle soloists were joined by dancers, such as John Diamond, whose combination of black gestures and Scottish/Irish jigs delighted the crowds.

By today's standards, the stereotypes and heavy caricatures of minstrel music are offensive. At the time they were in vogue, however, they did "humanize" the black man and present him as a comic hero, albeit limited in emotional scope and vision. The minstrel songs also created an American musical type and performing style that punctured pomposity and lampooned the pretentiously arty and the fawning over imported virtuosi. In minstrelsy, Americans truly had the beginnings of their own indigenous music, which would lead in time to ragtime, then jazz, and eventually rock-and-roll.

After the 1870s, minstrelsy began to change character. It tended to variety and foreshadowed the vulgarities of vaudeville and burlesque. Ironically, black performers now began appearing on stage in blackface. The only really notable composer of the late period, James A. Bland, wrote "Carry Me Back to Old Virginny" (1878), "In the Evening by the Moonlight" (1880), and "Oh, dem Golden Slippers" (1879). The minstrel period was over, but its spirit lived on and influenced such later performers as Eddie Cantor and Al Jolson. America finally had its own voice to sing with.

The original Jim Crow, Thomas "Daddy" Rice, in blackface, c. 1829. *Collection of Lawrence Zimmerman*

A popular song libretto from one of Dockstader's shows—one of the last minstrel companies—which included walk arounds as well as sentimental, comic, and "coon" songs.

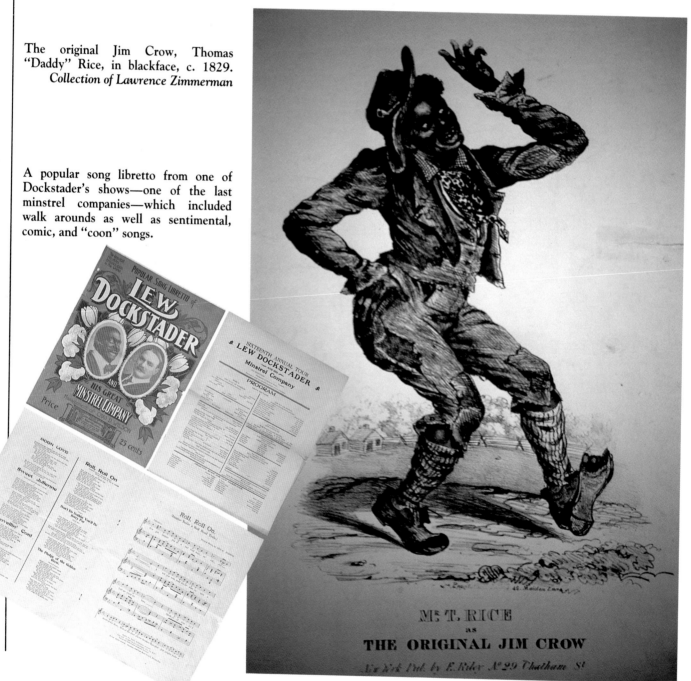

"A Hundred Years Hence"

SONGS OF PROTEST

SONGS OF PROTEST HAVE EXISTED from the earliest periods of American history. The oppressed have always sung of their discontent, and the belief and expectation of a better life have always been part of the American tradition.

Early music reflected the spirit of liberty and the desire for freedom from tyranny. This was made manifest in such songs as "In Freedom We're Born" (1768), which sounded the rousing call: "Come join hand in hand, brave Americans all,/ And rouse your bold hearts at fair Liberty's call,/ No tyrannous acts shall suppress your just claim,/ Nor stain with dishonor America's name." "The Revolutionary Alpha-

Slaves were not thought of as human beings but rather as "contraband." This rare cover (1861) shows a slave catcher after his prey. *Collection of Dr. Danny O. Crew*

bet" began: "A stands for Americans who never will be slaves./ B's for Boston's bravery that ever freedom saves./ C is for the Congress, which, though loyal, will be free./ D stands for defense against all force and tyranny./ Stand firmly A to Z/ We swear forever to be free!"

The Declaration of Independence inspired hundreds of commentaries in song. "Independence Day," the work of Dr. Jonathan M. Sewall of New Hampshire, went, in part: "George the Third of Great Britain no longer shall reign,/ With unlimited sway o'er these free states again; Lord North, nor old Bute, nor none of their clan,/ Shall ever hold sway o'er an American." "Chester," by America's earliest native-born composer, William Billings, became the New Englanders' favorite hymn of freedom.

"Fare Thee Well, You Sweethearts" was sung by Washington's troops as the war drew to an end. It reflected in its upbeat lyrics the longing for peace in the colonies: "The rising world shall sing of us a thousand years to come,/ And tell our children's children of the wonders we have done,/ And when the war is over we will set us down at ease,/ And plow and sow and reap and mow, and live just as we please,/ And then each lad shall take his lass all beaming like a star,/ And in her loving arms forget the dangers of the war . . ."

On July 3, 1776, the *Pennsylvania Gazette* announced: "Yesterday the Continental Congress declared the United Colonies Free and Independent States." The rejoicing took the form of songs, among which was one from the *New York Packet* sung to the tune of "God Save the King": "Hail! O America!/ Hail now the joyful day!/ Exalt your voice./ Shout, George is King no more,/ Over this Western shore; Let him his loss deplore,/ While we rejoice."

On October 17, 1781, when Cornwallis surrendered, newspapers reported that "the army played up Yankey doodle [*sic*], when the British army marched to lay down their arms."

Other protest and reform movements developed during the latter quarter of the eighteenth and first half of the nineteenth centuries, and most had songs sung about them, usually appearing as broadsides rather than sheet music. These reform demands included the movement for a shorter working day, end-ing discrimination against the immigrant Irish, and various labor and antimonopoly movements. Songs such as "Every Man His Own Politician," "Six to Six," and "No Irish Need Apply" reflected the sentiments of followers.

During the eighteenth century, a social conscience had been the province of the humanitarian rich. By the 1830s, however, it had been adopted by the middle class. During the populist era of President Andrew Jackson, appeals were made to the masses, stressing that everyone was entitled to the same privileges enjoyed by the inherited wealthy or political elite.

Given this atmosphere, America's acceptance of slavery seemed to some a serious national moral lapse, and led reformers to scrutinize the morality of other social institutions as well. Women argued that their lives were similar to those of slaves, and that they suffered increasingly from the drunkenness of men. "Temperance provided a certain respectability to the abolitionists who were ever being termed fanatics," as Nancy Knox Hancock has pointed out, and a pattern of interdependence was established among antislavery, temperance, and women's rights movements.

Slavery was a phenomenon as old as the colonies in North American territory. As early as 1619, a Dutch ship docked at the English colony of Jamestown, Virginia, with a group of slaves that were purchased outright by the colonists. By the outbreak of the Civil War, there were an estimated 4.5 million slaves in the United States, a staggering number of human lives trapped in an overwhelming tragedy.

No other immigrant group shares the unique situation of the black slave. When others—German, Irish, Dutch, English—came to America, it was to live as free men and women in a free land, finally able to pursue their personal, religious, and professional dreams unfettered by the chains of former political or social repression. If these individuals entered into the service of another, it was for a brief time only—done in order to pay passage, buy land, or get a start in the New World. However, the shiploads of blacks that continued to cross the oceans were brought for one express purpose—to be sold forever into the service of another.

Other immigrant groups retained many of their customs, their cultural heritage, and their unique traditions. Blacks, on the other hand, were the victims of cultural obliteration. Tribes and families were separated. The old ways could be no more.

Forced into long hours of servitude in clearing and working the land to develop the new continent,

Left: A little girl longs for happier days before she was known as the drunkard's child (1870). *Right:* The plight of a poor woman and her children, trapped outside in the cold because father is too drunk to let them in.

blacks began to create their own new and unique culture. And this culture was to be reflected in song.

First, there was the basis of African rhythms—complex concepts encompassing several patterns in one musical statement. Then, New World hymn and psalm influences were added. Finally, the deeply heartfelt sorrows of a life of misery coupled with new-found faith in the freedom of eternal life produced some of the most moving songs, songs that were all a part of the burgeoning black slave culture in the New World. These songs provided a unity of spirit that was much needed and was to be of crucial importance in the eventual quest for freedom. This longing for freedom was often expressed through biblical allusion, as in "Go Down Moses."

The plight of slaves did not go unrecognized. Antislavery songs appeared soon after the Revolutionary War. A song published in Rhode Island in 1792 was a plea for universal brotherhood: "Whatever harm dare in shape or make,/ What harm in ugly feature?/ Whatever colour, form he take,/ *de soul make human creature.*" Published in *The American Musical Miscellany* in 1798 was "The Desponding Negro," a song about the kidnapping and sale into bondage of an African slave. Another song title of the 1790s was "I Sold a Weeping Negro Boy."

In 1793, legislation was passed that was repugnant to Northerners, Quakers, free blacks, and other antislavery groups. The First Fugitive Slave Law ordered the return of slaves seeking refuge in states other than their own. Waves of debate on the ramifications of this legislation were still being heard in 1850 when such notable figures as Henry Clay, John C. Calhoun, Daniel Webster, Stephen Douglas, and Jefferson Davis hotly aired their views.

slavery until 1820, although they did little to curtail its practice. When cotton production rose, however, so did widespread Southern support for slavery. The road to the underground seemed more and more attractive.

The term *underground* was coined when Tice Davids fled across the Ohio River with his master in hot pursuit. On the other side, the runaway's helpers covered his tracks so well that the frustrated owner concluded that Davids must have "gone on an underground road." Thereafter, the term grew to Underground Railroad, with appropriate accompanying terms such as *conductor* and *track*. Former slaves, such as Harriet Tubman, figured prominently in helping others to escape through these routes.

The song "Underground Rail Car, or Song of the Fugitive," written and composed by George N. Allen, was published by Oliver Ditson in 1854. Its black-and-white cover picture shows a black slave carrying a pack on a stick and approaching a steam train. The song declared: "I'm on my way to Canada a freeman's rights to share./ The cruel wrongs of slavery/ I can no longer bear. . . . O dear friends, haste and follow,/ For I am safe

In response to the 1793 law, those advocating the abolition of slavery constructed throughout the Northeast a cooperative system that came to be called the Underground Railroad. In effect, it was a blanket whereunder a slave might be hidden from his captors and eventually escape.

Responsible Southerners were verbally condemning

A "contraband" cover, *top*, executed toward the end of the Civil War. Soon the laws making human beings "goods and chattel" would be revoked. *Collection of Dr. Danny O. Crew*

Cordelia Howard, a popular child star (c. 1853) as The Gentle Eva in *Uncle Tom's Cabin*, *above*, a dramatic musical rendering of the book that catapulted the movement for abolition into the national consciousness.

Below right: A comic song from 1840 whose subject is a temperance meeting. Published by Henry Prentiss Publishers. *Collection of Lawrence Zimmerman*

Above: A sarcastic ditty lampooning the suffrage movement in which a father explains to his children that mother has gone away to join the "suffrage army."

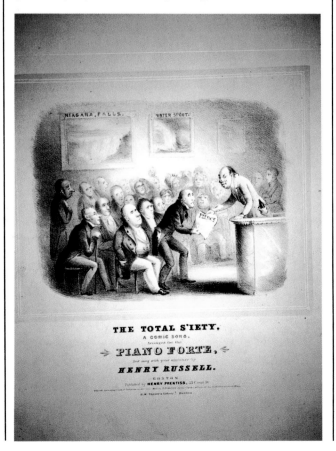

in Canada, where the panting slave is free!"

The song was dedicated to former slave Frederick Douglass, who escaped to become one of the most impressive supporters of the antislavery movement. His moving speeches at his church in New Bedford, Massachusetts, attracted William Lloyd Garrison, famous abolitionist and editor of *The Liberator*, who sent Douglass on a lecture tour to speak for freedom.

Theodore Dwight Weld led another abolitionist group that was strongly opposed to Garrison's tactics. Weld published a pamphlet of documented horror tales of slavery called *American Slavery As It Is.* It was said to have influenced the writing of *Uncle Tom's Cabin.*

During the 1840s and 1850s, minstrel shows faced competition from singing families. The most popular of these were the Hutchinsons. They were New Hampshire siblings whose parents had had sixteen children, nearly all of them musical. The Hutchinsons saw themselves as missionaries for the downtrodden, and through song they tirelessly reiterated their stands on political and moral issues such as abolition, woman suffrage, and temperance. Until the Civil War, they exerted a major influence on American thinking on behalf of abolition. "Get Off the Track," sung by the Hutchinsons in 1844, was a dynamic allegory comparing emancipation to the new and unstoppable energy of the railroads. The sheet-music cover featured a railroad car named "Immediate Emancipation," flags, and a crowd, and chorused: "Roll it along, thro' the Nation/Freedom's Car, Emancipation." The Hutchinsons also wrote, in 1844, a song for James Birney, presidential candidate for the abolitionist Liberty Party titled, "We're for Freedom Through the Land." A slave song that concerned itself with the Underground Railroad was "The Drinking Gourd." The song, of hidden meaning, was a map of the local branch line of the Underground Railroad and the "Drinking Gourd" was the constellation Big Dipper—which points north.

In 1848, a booklet entitled "The Anti-Slavery Harp: Collection of Songs for Anti-Slavery Meetings," compiled by William W. Brown, a fugitive slave, was published in Boston by Bela Marsh. It was, said Brown, a response to demands by the public for a cheap antislavery songbook and contained such songs as "Have We Not All One Father?" "O, Pity the Slave Mother," "The Blind Slave Boy," "Ye Songs of Freemen" (sung to the tune of "The Marseilles"), "Freedom's Star," and "The Liberty Ball" (to the tune of "Rosin the Bow").

Harriet Beecher Stowe, daughter of an ardent abolitionist, added more impact to the sentiments of anti-slavery through her book *Uncle Tom's Cabin* than did any other group, speech, publication, or campaign. The book saw forms of theatrical production, including one starring Cordelia Howard, the Shirley Temple of her day, as Little Eva. Numerous songs were associated with the production. "I am Going There, or the Death of Little Eva" and "Little Eva, Uncle Tom's Guardian Angel" were among them. Other characters were too popular to be ignored by songwriters: "Eliza's Flight" showed a black-and-white picture of Eliza and her baby caught on the ice, and "Oh, I'se So Wicked" was Topsy's song.

Elizabeth Cady Stanton, Susan B. Anthony, and Lucretia Mott were also actively involved in antislavery campaigns and activities. Stanton and Anthony organized the Women's National Loyal League in 1853 to support the Union. Susan B. Anthony organized a memorial meeting for John Brown, the leader of the famous raid on Harper's Ferry. The resulting funds went to Brown's widow and children. "John Brown's Body" became a noted song with numerous texts, including an abolitionist setting by Edna Dean Proctor. Anthony and Stanton led the Women's Central Committee proclamation in 1863, which stated that true peace in the republic would come about only when all of its subjects were equal.

Emancipation from slavery was to come. For some it was through escape. "No more auction block for me" is a line from "Many Thousand Gone," a popular song sung by slaves who fled as far north as Canada's Nova Scotia. For some it was through the hope of eternal freedom: "And before I'll be a slave,/ I'll lie buried in my grave,/ And go home to my Lord and—be free." And for some, it was through the ultimate gains of conflict. "We are coming from the cottonfields, We are coming from afar;/ We have left the plough, the hoe, the ore,/ And we are going to war," cried "Song of the Freedmen."

Songs of peace finally rang out at the end of the Civil War and reflected the demise of the evils of officially sanctioned slavery and the hope for a future of peace and brotherhood. "For the people are all free;/ And the Jubilee hath sounded—/ Universal Liberty" went part of a song published for the first postwar July Fourth celebration. Such peace, of course, eluded the citizens of the postwar era. Sadly, the agony of Reconstruction and the bitterness of the South precluded a truly reunited country until the end of the nineteenth century.

The evils of drink had long been chronicled in American story, song, and political debate. For all those who spoke out against the "demon rum," there were as many who spoke in favor of the pleasures of "ardent spirits." And there were those who gave the illusion of piety but carried the secret hip flask. Church groups traditionally sponsored moderation in drink, but civic and political platforms drew more notice.

Records as early as 1789 show that two hundred farmers in Litchfield, Connecticut, banded together into a temperance society, pledging not to provide any strong drink for their workmen. (Although they said nothing about themselves.)

Massachusetts was the scene of many a hot debate over strong drink between those of staunch Puritan tradition and those who liked a "good time," particularly during the 1830s. Finally, in 1838, this state passed a law banning the sale of "ardent spirits" of less than fifteen gallons in quantity—fifteen gallons or more had to be purchased and delivered at one time.

However, one enterprising Yankee got a license to exhibit his pig—which he had painted with red and

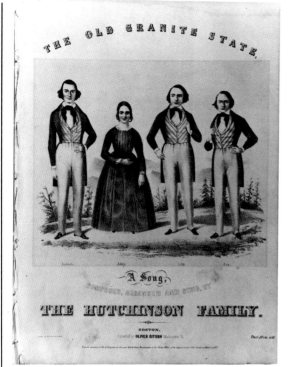

The Singing Hutchinson Family sang this song (1843), which refers to both abolition and temperance and includes the words "Yes, we're friends of emancipation" and "liberty is our motto," a reference to the Liberty Party, the party of abolitionism. *Collection of Kurt Stein*

Right: A Currier lithograph of the famous 1840 song. *Collection of Lawrence Zimmerman*

black stripes—in a tent on a muster field in Dedham, Massachusetts. Word soon spread that included with the price of admission was a free glass of grog. The story of this early American "scofflaw" was told in the song entitled "The Striped Pig." One verse sums up the ingenuity of the pig's master whereby he "hit on a plan a little bit slicker/ By which he could furnish these soldiers with liquor."

Even though the fifteen-gallon law was repealed in 1840, that did not mark an end to the move toward a more temperant society, or to the fun poked at its advocates.

In 1836, the tune "Think and Smoke Tobacco" sported a cover engraving showing the hazards of overindulgence in drinking and smoking. Serious temperance societies sprouting up around the country warned of overindulgence in drink as portrayed in these songs. By midcentury, many of the groups were demanding the passage of temperance legislation, protesting that something must be done to curtail the evil that was ruining the fabric of home and family.

A National Temperance Society organized many state and local groups. Warriors of temperance, or teetotalism as it was called, spread their message in halls and on street corners, taking drunks out of the gutter and handing them the "pledge."

In order to appease the semi-inebriated audiences and spare them the boredom of long speeches and lectures, shrewd leaders sprinkled their meetings with popular songs and hymns to which they added temperance texts. This tactic got their message across in a pleasant and memorable way. "Woodman, Spare That Tree" became "Drunkard, Spare That Cup" or "Young Man, Shun That Cup." "Auld Lang Syne" was transformed into "Te-totallers Auld Lang Syne": "Be days of drinking wine forgot,/ Let water goblets shine—/ And from your memory ever blot/ The days of drinking wine" (published in *Cold Water Melodies*). Even the "Star-Spangled Banner" turned into the "National Temperance Ode" in 1840.

Songs dedicated to reformed drunkards provided powerful publicity for the cause. John Gough signed

This cover celebrates the vote won in four states as the movement marches on. *Collection of Dr. Danny O. Crew*

A song cover (1913) designed to rally support for the suffrage movement. *Collection of Dr. Danny O. Crew*

the pledge in 1842 after a life of wandering and drinking. He was an eloquent speaker who could pack the house with his testimony. "A Cup of Water" was dedicated to him. "For bright his eye, and his spirit high," it ran, "Who drinks but the clear cold water."

It was tempting to take a cynical view of these proceedings. Henry Russell was noted for his amusing impressions of the pious hypocrite with a flask in his pocket. "The Total S'iety," one famous song that he performed, had an interesting story to tell: "One night I'd been lecturing hard/ I felt that my breathing grew shorter/ I found that some wag 'pon my word/ Had put Gin in my pitcher of Water."

In 1850, Mrs. Amelia Bloomer popularized a new dress option for women. The style was enthusiastically supported by women's rights activists, who believed that a corseted body meant a corseted mind.

"The Tee-to-tal Society" tells the tale of a poor soul who left his healthy, jovial cup of brew for the sterner road of the pledge. He dies unhappy and thin —"His inside was stuffed full of Tea Leaves and Snow Balls."

Although men initiated the temperance campaign, women joined it in droves. When temperance became a women's issue and thereby linked with home and family, songwriters seized upon the sentimental possibilities and became adept at portraying the downtrodden wife and the fatherless child. Songs such as "Papa Don't Drink Any More," in which a young daughter struggles to drag her father from a saloon, "Come Home Father," and "Father Drinks No More" were tearjerkers guaranteed to stir the hearts of even the most fervent "wets."

Dr. Dio Lewis, a temperance speaker in Hillsboro, Ohio, is credited with helping to inspire the National Women's Campaign. Subsequently, Mother Stewart led the Ohio Women's Temperance Crusade, which grew into the Women's Christian Temperance Union, dedicated to maintaining the sanctity of home and family. Susan B. Anthony and Amelia Bloomer

E. T. Paull's brilliant cover, *right*, depicting the spirit and idealism of the women's suffrage movement (1916).

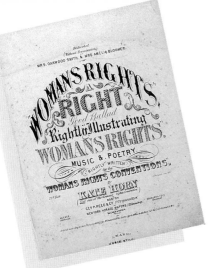

were strong advocates of temperance, and worked ardently for this cause along with abolition and suffrage.

In 1853, a so-called world's convention on temperance was held in New York. The atmosphere was highly charged and moved to the point of hysteria, whereupon it was ruled that it was immoral for women to speak in public on the issue of temperance—or any issue, for that matter. Outraged, the women in attendance withdrew to fight their own campaign. They were roundly supported by a certain Mr. Townsend, a wealthy manufacturer of sarsaparilla.

Public sentiments were running high, and so were the songs. "Speed, Speed the Temperance Ship," " 'Tis But a Drop," "The Dying Drunkard," "The First Pledge," and "They Called Me Drunken Roarer" are among a few of those that commemorated the movement's efforts. Ultimately, prohibition legislation was passed for a time just before the outbreak of the Civil War. However, the debates raged on long after.

"Crooked Whiskey" (which dealt with the goings-on of the notorious Whiskey Ring), "Empty Is the Bottle, Father's Tight," and "I'll Never Get Drunk Any More," all of the 1870s, were echoes of the heyday of the early temperance movement. But they led to other songs after the turn of the century such as "Come Down and Pick Your Husband Out (The Rest of Us Want to Go Home)," and "What'll We Do on a Saturday Night (When the Town Goes Dry)." This new generation of songs foreshadowed the troubled era of Prohibition that began with the passage of the Eighteenth Amendment to the Constitution in 1919.

Although the repeal of Prohibition in 1933 showed temperance to be a failed experiment, the cause of woman suffrage eventually triumphed. American women had begun agitating for equality at home and in the ballot box as early as the seventeenth century. According to song historian Irwin Silber, Margaret Brent appeared before the Maryland House of Burgesses in 1647 and demanded the right to vote. Anne

Hutchinson's battle with the elders of the Massachusetts Bay Colony for a voice in church affairs in 1637 was also a suffrage demand.

In 1795, the *Philadelphia Minerva* published a song called "Rights of Woman" by "an anonymous Lady," to the tune of "God Save the King." As radical a demand for equality as anything written since, it chorused: "Man boasts the noble cause,/ Nor yields supine to laws,/ Tyrants ordain;/ Let woman have a share,/ Nor yield to slavish fear,/ Her equal rights declare,/ And well maintain."

In New Jersey, from 1776 to 1807, women and blacks voted the same as white men. Considered by some to be a ploy by the Federalists to pad ballot boxes, this step inspired a satiric song, "The Freedom of Election," the last chorus of which went: "Then Freedom hail!—thy powers prevail/ O'er prejudice and error;/ No longer shall men tyrannize/ And rule the world in terror:/Now one and all, proclaim the fall/ Of tyrants!—Open wide your throats,/ And welcome in the Peaceful Scene/ Of government in petticoats!"

In 1851, inspired by her friendship with Elizabeth Cady Stanton and Susan B. Anthony, Mrs. Amelia Bloomer of Seneca Falls promoted the wearing of trousers by women in her newspaper *The Lily.* The "bloomer" style inspired a number of tunes, including "The Bloomers' Complaint," which went in part: "Dear me, what a terrible clatter they raise,/ Because that old gossip Dame Rumor/ Declares with her hands lifted up in amaze/ That I'm coming out as a Bloomer. . . . I wonder how often these men must be told. . . . / However they ridicule, lecture or scold/ She'll do after all, as she pleases."

The singing group the Hutchinsons also raised their voices for woman suffrage, believing that when women got the vote they would bring a new morality to bear in the battle for reform. When the Hutchinsons sang the militant feminist "Let Us All Speak Our Minds If We Die for It," it inspired wild support as well as furious contempt with lines such as "Let man if he will then bid us be still,/ And silent, a price he'll pay high for it—/ For we won't and we can't, and we don't and we shan't,/ Let us all speak our minds if we die for it!"

In 1835, a blow was struck for feminism with the publication of "I'll Be No Submissive Wife." The song, which stated, "I'll be no submissive wife. . . . I'll not be a slave for life," must have been popular, since it went into innumerable editions.

A parody on Stephen Foster's Civil War song "We Are Coming Father Abraam" was written and sung at an Elizabeth Cady Stanton birthday celebration in

Wisconsin. It was titled "We Are Coming Mother Stanton," and chorused: "We are coming! We are coming!/ The ballot to obtain;/ We are coming Mother Stanton,/ With all our might and main;/ We are coming Mother Stanton,/ A long and valiant train. . . . / We will not look behind us,/ But steadfastly before;/ We are coming Mother Stanton,/ A million women more."

In 1867, the Hutchinsons sang for the first organized campaign for suffrage in Kansas, where a referendum was on the ballot. To the tune of "Old Dan Tucker," John W. Hutchinson and P. P. Fowler wrote: "Oh, say what thrilling songs of fairies,/ Wafted o'er the Kansas prairies,/ Charm the ear while zephyrs speed 'em,/ Woman's pleading for her freedom."

In 1869, two woman suffrage conventions met in Chicago. Reaction to this organized women's movement consisted mainly of indignation and ridicule. A "comic" song titled "We'll Show You When We Come to Vote," written by Frank Howard, pictured women as vain, selfish creatures—and men as not much better. The cover portrayed women casting their ballots surrounded by signs featuring names of prominent suffrage leaders as well as one reading: DOWN WITH MALE RULE.

In 1872, Victoria Woodhull's campaign for president as a candidate of the Equal Rights Party was promoted by songs such as the "Grundys," which attempted to lay to rest prudery in its worst form and promote the team of Woodhull and Frederick Douglass. Douglass, however, declined to run with her.

A sarcastic ballad called "Rights of Ladies" capitalized not only on the issue of woman suffrage but on prejudice against waves of Irish immigration. A chorus went: "And whin all the votin' is over,/ An' Biddy's elected, shure thin/ I'll live like a pig in the clover/ Wid Honorable Misses McFlinn."

Other suffrage songs written during the last quarter of the nineteenth century include "Going to the Polls," which indicated women's intentions to use the ballot for social and moral reform; "Oh, Dear What Can the Matter Be," sung to the tune of the same name, which asked the question, "Oh, Dear, what can the matter be?/When men want every vote?"; and "The Taxation Tyranny," which evoked memories of the American Revolution with its stirring verse "So, as woman is punished for breaking/ The laws which she cannot gainsay/ Let us give her a voice in the making,/ Or ask her no more to obey."

The publicity given the woman suffrage movement in England, along with New Jersey activist Alice Paul's tales of her arrest and force-feeding, inspired the songwriting team of J. J. Gallagher and B. A. Koelhoffer to write "Oh! You Suffragettes" in 1912. The title page featured a parade of girls carrying a banner reading VOTES FOR WOMEN. In the background a woman heaves bricks through a window.

Other songs written in the early part of the century included "Winning the Vote" by Mrs. A. B. Smith, and a "comic sad" tale by Thomas Gray and Raymond Walker entitled "Your Mother's Gone Away to Join the Army"—the suffrage army, that is. Olive Drennan wrote a spunky song, "I'm a Suffragette," about the "new" woman in 1912 who insists on the right to vote before she will consider marriage. D. Estabrook, the author of the earlier "Taxation Tyranny," also wrote "Keep Woman in Her Sphere," which ended with the plea, "Her rights are just the same as mine,/ Let woman choose her sphere." And Lucenia W. Richards wrote "Suffrage March" in 1914; its title page depicts a woman bearing a banner with the words UNIVERSAL SUFFRAGE on it.

By 1917, when President Woodrow Wilson still had not endorsed equal suffrage, women besieged the White House. For three months, day after day, the pickets tried to secure an audience with the president, but to no avail. Many of the protesters were arrested, imprisoned, and, when they went on hunger strikes, force-fed. After the United States became involved in World War I, suffragists continued to remind Congress and President Wilson that women's efforts were contributing to the winning of the war abroad as well as to maintenance of peace on the home front. The Nineteenth Amendment, giving women the vote, was finally enacted in 1920.

Abolition, temperance, woman suffrage, workers' rights, immigration woes—Americans sang about them all.

In 1876, at a woman suffrage convention, the Hutchinson family sang "A Hundred Years Hence." Written by Frances Dana Gage, it joyously predicted a utopian world where there would be no wrongs to right:

Then woman, man's partner, man's equal shall
   stand,
While beauty and harmony govern the land. . . .
Oppression and war will be heard of no more,
Nor the blood of a slave have its print on our
   shore. . . .

It seems we have a ways to go. Although this song is a relic of our past, it is also a reminder that dreams die hard, that some never die at all, and that one of the best ways to keep a dream alive is with a song.

"Wake Nicodemus"

SONGS OF THE CIVIL WAR

No period of American history is more profoundly moving than the Civil War. It created more passion, heartache, and bitterness than any other. As brother fought brother and the country was rent asunder by institutionalized fratricide, there was an outpouring of popular songs. More than ten thousand songs were inspired by the Civil War, and the greatest of them are still sung today. Sheet-music cover art, as well, reached a heretofore unseen pinnacle of patriotism that would not reappear until World War I.

The songs that the soldiers sang in camp and in battle, and the ones sung at home by their loved ones, reflected two hundred years of America's developing music and a subsequent American style: evangelical, an amalgam of Negro and white spirituals; minstrel tunes; Stephen Foster melodies; psalmbooks; singing schools; hymnals; and foreign folk songs. This distinctly developed melodic style is still beloved today,

for do we not still know and sing "Tenting Tonight," "Tramp, Tramp, Tramp," "Aura Lea" ("Love Me Tender"), and "Battle Hymn of the Republic"?

The two greatest and most prolific composers connected with this period were George Frederick Root and Henry Clay Work. Root wrote his first song about the war three days after the firing on Fort Sumter. He called it "The First Gun Is Fired." In 1861, he wrote a stirring call for courage called "Forward, Boys, Forward," and with it his first sentimental ballad, "The Vacant Chair." The war was still young in 1861, but enough families had already lost loved ones for the song to affect many, in both the North and the South.

Root's greatest song, one of the classics of the Civil War, appeared in 1862. It was called "The Battle Cry of Freedom" or "We'll Rally 'Round the Flag." It was introduced in New York by the Hutchinsons, and quickly soared to popularity. Within two years of its first publication, 350,000 copies of the sheet music had been sold. Root also wrote the well-known "Tramp, Tramp, Tramp" in 1863, the most successful song on the subject of war prisoners. Also published at this time was Root's sentimental "Just Before the Battle, Mother."

Henry Clay Work, a passionate abolitionist, was the only other composer to rival Root in the production of Civil War classics. In 1862, he wrote "Kingdom Coming," an antislavery song in Negro dialect. "Wake Nicodemus," written in 1864, also contained pronounced abolitionist feeling. Work's greatest effort and most passionate song was his masterpiece, "Marching Through Georgia," written in 1864 to commemorate William Tecumseh Sherman's march to the sea, which spelled doom for the South. The song does have a dark, cruel side and, until very recently, could still stir anger in the breast of even the most modern Southern lady or gentleman.

The most popular rallying songs were, of course, "Dixie" and "The Battle Hymn of the Republic." As a Northerner, Daniel Decatur Emmett had a difficult time explaining that he did not compose "Dixie" for the war. However, its popularity caught on after it was played at Jefferson Davis's inauguration as president of the Confederate states in Montgomery, Ala-

A stirring Civil War/Abolition song by fervent abolitionist Henry Clay Work.

Right: One of the most popular songs of the Civil War.

LORENA

And hear the distant Church bells chimed.

For "if we try we may forge

But there, up there, 'tis Heart to Heart.

Guitar.

Piano.

CHRGOTT, FORBRIGER & Co. LITH CINCINNATI.

CHICAGO.
Published by H.M. HIGGINS, 117 Randolph St.

Left: Mournful dirge for Abraham Lincoln written after his assassination. *Collection of Kurt Stein*

Right: Sentimental ballad commemorating one of the Civil War's beloved drummer boys. *Collection of Kurt Stein*

bama, in 1861. It soon came to symbolize the Confederacy—not exactly what Emmett had intended. When the tune of "Dixie" became the official Southern battle hymn, it was set to warlike words by many different Confederate authors.

"The Battle Hymn of the Republic" took its tune from "Say Brothers, Will You Meet Us?" an 1850s black camp meeting song. It was Julia Ward Howe who added the stirring and unforgettable words.

Numerous other rallying songs were written to charge the spirits of those off to war as well as those contemplating joining in. Perhaps the most recognized of these "volunteer" songs was Stephen Foster's "We Are Coming, Father Abraam." It served as a vote of support to President Lincoln's call for 300,000 additional volunteers:

> *We're coming, Father Abraam*
> *One hundred thousand more*
> *Five hundred presses printing us*
> *From morn till night is o'er.*

The South rallied with such tunes as "The Volunteer; or, It is My Country's Call" and "Bonnie Blue Flag." The chorus of the latter went:

> *Hurrah! Hurrah! for Southern rights, hurrah!*
> *Hurrah for the bonnie blue flag that bears a*
> *single star.*

The North responded to this with words of its own. The song was introduced in 1861 by its author, Harry Macarthy. The first-edition cover bears crossed flags and a dedication to General Albert Pike. The tune was a jig from the 1850s, "The Irish Jaunting Car."

Another important Southern song that had a bor-

rowed tune was "Maryland, My Maryland," written by James R. Randall and set to the German tune "Tannenbaum, O Tannenbaum." The cover of the first edition bears the Maryland coat of arms. The names of author and arranger were omitted, as the song was highly subversive with its references to "patriotic gore" and "Northern scum."

Obviously, "The Star-Spangled Banner" figured prominently in the Northern repertoire of patriotic songs. The South used the tune but added the words that became "Cross of the South."

The black population added significantly to the song literature of the military call to arms. "De Darkies' Rallying Song," "A Soldier in de Colored Brigade," and "We Are Coming from the Cotton Fields" are among a few of these tributes to black soldiers who helped support military efforts. In addition to the sheet music issued for many of these songs, broadsides and "words only" pocket songsters also appeared.

Root's "The First Gun is Fired! May God Protect the Right!" was published both in sheet music and in broadside. Songsters proliferated on both sides of the Mason-Dixon line. *Knapsack Songster, Union Song Book,* and the *Red, White, and Blue Songster* kept Northern soldiers and supporters singing to familiar tunes. Confederate counterparts included *Hopkins' New Orleans 5 Cent Song Book, Songs of the South,* and *New Confederate Flag Song Book.*

As soon as the South seceded from the Union, it began creating and using its own songs instead of Northern ones. "The Palmetto State Song" was issued only a few days after secession, and many others followed. This was a remarkable accomplishment, since the South lacked type, ink, and paper in large quantities. Type fonts were smuggled from the North through Union lines, and as ink grew scarcer the print grew fainter on published pieces. When paper supplies dwindled, Confederates experimented with new ways to produce paper, even using cotton. Eventually, dingy and cramped sheet-music scores resulted. Yet the South proudly supported its cause through music despite the harrowing odds.

Songs representing the political factionalism of the time also proliferated. In 1860, Stephen A. Douglas was nominated for president on the Democratic ticket. He was a fence sitter on slavery who had angered both the North and South, so much so that some Southerners nominated John C. Breckinridge for the presidency instead. The Republicans, of course, nominated Abraham Lincoln.

The Lincoln songs of 1860 contained strongly forthright and militant sentiments. The bloody strife in Kansas had proved that compromise with the slave system was impossible, and the Republican stand was to disallow its extension into new states and territories. Songs like "Freemen Win When Lincoln Leads," "Lincoln and Liberty" (words by Jesse Hutchinson), and "Lincoln and Hamlin" reflected this spirit.

Songs that supported Douglas in the North, as well as Breckinridge and John Bell (of the Know-Nothing party) in the South, included "Stand By the Flag," "Breckinridge and Lane," and "Union Dixie." "Get Out of the Way," sung to the tune of "Old Dan Tucker," pinned the "woolly-head" label on the Republicans, mostly to appeal to prejudice against blacks. Its chorus went: "Get out of the way now, all seceders,/ And woolly-head Disunion leaders."

By 1864, Americans had divided sharply into two camps for what was in effect a referendum on the war. The Democratic candidate for president was Gen. George B. McClellan, onetime commander of the Army of the Potomac, who had been removed by Lincoln for failure to enthusiastically wage war. Many songs written and sung on behalf of the Democratic nominees were ugly and racist in their proslavery fervor. "White Soldiers' Song" went, in part:

Tell Abe Lincoln to let the nigger be,
Tell Abe Lincoln that we don't want him free. . . .
Tell Abe Lincoln of Antietam's bloody dell,
Tell Abe Lincoln where a thousand heroes fell,
Tell Abe Lincoln and his gang to go to hell.

To the melodies of popular songs like "Wait For the Wagon," pro-slave system songs proliferated. Some attacked an act of Congress that resulted in the recruitment of tens of thousands of black soldiers for the Union army. Other songs that supported McClellan included "McClellan Is the Man," "Soon We'll Have the Union Back," "Little Mac Shall Be Restored," and "Little Mac! Little Mac! You're the Very Man."

Songs supporting Lincoln's campaign included "Rally 'Round the Cause, Boys," "Rally for Old Abe," and "Union Coming." The latter, to the tune of "Kingdom Coming," chorused:

For Maine has said, Ha! Ha!
Vermont she say, Ho! Ho!
We'll sing de song ob Union eber,
From Maine to Mexico!

Stories of battles, victories, and heroes naturally found their way into song for both the Blue and the Grey. "The Sword of Robert E. Lee," "Jefferson Davis," and "General Beauregard's Grand March" heralded the Confederacy. "The Southern Girl" portrayed the fierce pride that Southerners showed in support of their heroes and their cause:

My homespun dress is plain, I know,
My hat's palmetto, too,
But, then, it shows what Southern girls
For Southern rights will do.

Soldiers and leaders who became famous during the Civil War had their fame reflected in song: "Sherman the Brave," "Honor to Sheridan," "Stonewall Jackson's Way," "Beauregard," and "Riding a Raid (A Tribute to J.E.B. Stuart)" are examples of this genre.

The John Brown for whom the "John Brown Song" was named was not the martyr of Harper's Ferry but a Sergeant John Brown who served in a Massachusetts volunteer regiment. The song's lyrics were communally improvised to an old Methodist hymn and finally published in 1861 as a broadside. Sixty-five different sheet-music editions of it were published.

Heroines were not left unsung either. "Jenny Wade, the Heroine of Gettysburg" is an example.

Emotional preparation for battle was chronicled in such works as "The Night Before the Battle" and "On the Eve of Battle, Sister." The North echoed the spirit of battle in "Comrades Hasten to the Battle" and "Leave Me and Save the Glorious Flag."

Behind the calls to arms and the shouts of patriotism, there was another side to the war, a distinctly human element. Families parted. Lovers said goodbye. Homes were destroyed. And precious sons were never to return again. The musical outpouring of these feelings had their expression around the campfire as well as the parlor piano.

The touching sentiment of these emotions shone

Left: Grand march honoring Philip Henry Sheridan, commander of the armies of the Potomac and the Shenandoah. The South never forgave his cruel and indiscriminate destruction of crops, livestock, and homes or his harsh reconstruction policy. *Collection of Kurt Stein*

Right: The anthem of the South during the Civil War (1862). *Collection of Kurt Stein*

RECONSTRUCTION!

AS IT SHOULD BE

AS IT IS!

Grand March

BY

CHARLES YOUNG.

Published by J. L. PETERS, 599 Broadway, N.Y.

through such songs as "Who Will Care For Mother Now?" by Charles Carroll Sawyer, "Was My Brother in the Battle?" by Stephen Foster, and "The Vacant Chair" by George Frederick Root.

The tragedy of dying soldiers was constantly emphasized, a universal grieving of Blue and Grey. Confederates sang "Kiss Me Before I Die, Mother." The dying Union soldier was portrayed in "Mother Kissed Me in My Dream." Other tragic songs were "The Soldier's Good-Bye," "Somebody's Darling," "The Southern Soldier Boy," "Mother Would Comfort Me," and "Foes and Friends," which portrays a soldier from New Hampshire and one from Georgia who, though foes by day, at night, dying, become friends.

Perhaps among the saddest of the sentimental war songs were those about the little drummer boys. "The Dying Drummer Boy" tells of a poor boy calling for his mother. "Little Major" recounts a tale of the drummer boy who is refused water by the enemy. And death comes for "Little Harry, the Drummer Boy."

Another memorable heart-rending song was "All Quiet Along the Potomac Tonight." The first-edition cover is dated 1864 and is dedicated to the "unknown dead of the present revolution." The first verse contains the heartbreaking lyrics:

> All quiet along the Potomac tonight,
> Except here and there a stray picket
> Is shot as he walks on his beat to and fro
> By a rifleman hid in the thicket.
> 'Tis nothing! A Private or two now and then
> Will not count in the news of battle.
> Not an officer lost!
> Only one of the men
> Moaning out all alone the death rattle.
> "All quiet along the Potomac tonight."

The song was very popular with both sides and eventually aroused public sympathy to such an extent that both armies issued orders prohibiting sniping at pickets.

The music covers for these melancholy songs evoke feelings of loss and hope through skillfully drawn scenes of parting, mourning, loneliness, and return. Other titles included "Dear Mother I've Come Home to Die," "Aura Lea," "Tell Mother I Die Happy," "When the Cruel War Is Over," "Lorena" (the "Annie Laurie" of the Confederate armies), "Never Forget the Dear Ones" by George F. Root, "The Yellow Rose of Texas" (a popular Confederate song), and "Weeping Sad and Lonely."

Left: **The hoped-for peace after the Civil War eluded both North and South as they struggled with the grim realities and disillusionment of the postwar era (1868).** *Collection of Dr. Danny O. Crew*

Sung by both sides in the Civil War, it has continued to be loved and sung until today.

A sentimental war song by the prolific George F. Root.

Stationed in New Orleans in 1863, Patrick S. Gelmore composed "When Johnny Comes Marching Home" under the pseudonym of Louis Lambert. It is an extraordinary musical legacy of the Civil War and still a classic. The first edition was published in 1863 by Henry Tolman and Company with a handsomely lettered cover ringed by stars.

Life was tough in the camps and on the marches, especially for young boys who had never been away from home before. Songs about everyday army life were often humorous, sometimes heartbreaking, and included "Hard Crackers Come Again No More" (to the tune of Stephen Foster's "Hard Times Come

Again No More''), which complained vociferously about the food given the Army of the Potomac; "Boys, Keep Your Powder Dry"; "Think of Your Head in the Morning," about excessive drinking by soldiers on both sides; "Here's Your Mule," which blames a farmer for troop desertion; "Short Rations," about Confederate soldiers forced to go into battle hungry; "Goober Peas," a Confederate nonsense song (soldiers from Georgia were called goobers, after peanuts); "Army Bugs"; and the great "Tenting on the Old Camp Ground," written by Walter Kittredge. This song's appeal was said to be so great on both sides that officers had to restrain their men from singing it at night in order not to give their positions away.

In 1864, as the Union came ever closer to winning the war, Jefferson Davis was taunted in a cruel Northern song, "How Do You Like It, Jefferson D.," published by Oliver Ditson, and "The Last Ditch Polka," which pictured Davis on the cover as a rat in a cage.

Davis was severely ridiculed in song by the North after the Southern surrender. He was supposed to have initially evaded capture by dressing in a disguise of women's clothing. This was, of course, fair game for a variety of songs with comic covers, among them "O, Jefferson Davis, How Do You Do?" "Jeff in Petticoats," and "Jeff Davis in Crinoline." "Goodbye, Jeff" and "Rebel Kingdom Falling" were not so much comic as commemorative of the nearing end.

Victory was indeed bittersweet for the North. Their beloved Abe Lincoln did not live long enough to savor the victory to the fullest. His untimely death was mourned appropriately in song. "Farewell, Father, Friend & Guardian" (music by George F. Root),

"We Mourn Our Fallen Chieftain," and "President Lincoln's Funeral March" (by T. M. Brown) are examples of music and cover art created to mark the memory of the fallen president.

Finally, the war ended. " 'Tis Finished," written by Henry Clay Work, and "Peace" by Charles Moulton celebrated the return of peace. Work's song ended with the chorus:

> *Then sing hallelujah;*
> *Glory be to God on high!*
> *For the old flag with the white flag*
> *Is hanging in the azure sky.*

The country was relieved that conflict had ended ("Our Boys Are Home to Stay" and "They Are Coming from the Wars"), but the aftermath of bitterness and destruction was to take a long time to mend. Reconstruction was far from an easy task. "Be Merciful to the South" and the black song "The Old Home Ain't What It Used to Be" reflect the hard adjustments that resulted.

The Civil War ripped apart the fabric of American society and plunged the country into a five-year torment of loss and lamentation. But as a direct result of this conflict, American popular music found its voice again, after having suffered through midcentury doldrums of overly sentimental torch songs and repetitive minstrelsy. When the war was over, more truly American music was being sung than ever before. And as a result of the emancipation of the slaves, the music of black suffering and hope was finally discovered and appreciated after two hundred years of obscurity.

"Silver Threads Among the Gold"

VICTORIAN STEREOTYPES

THE MAJORITY OF SONGS WRITTEN between the Civil War and the end of the nineteenth century mirrored, not the reality of the time with its agony of Reconstruction, mourning for fathers and sons, and rough-and-tumble politics, but instead, society's wish to bury its collective head in the sand while engaging in a narcotic orgy of sentimentality.

As the Victorian era unfolded, nostalgia became the byword of composers. Important contemporary issues were often ignored, while the separation of

spheres by gender and the deification of the home took firm root. American music of this period was, with a few exceptions, notably mediocre. Experimentation languished and music forms were rigid and repetitive.

With the separation of the spheres of home and industry brought about by the Industrial Revolution, an excessive idealization of women developed, especially in the East, which was the vanguard of the nation's cultural development. Women no longer had to be busy with the tasks of their colonial forebears. They now had leisure, money, and opportunity. The degree of a woman's idleness became a clue to her social position. This was true, of course, only of middle- and upper-class women; their working-class sisters lived lives of unceasing drudgery.

As men spent more and more time away from home, the home became exclusively the woman's domain. She became its mistress and the arbiter of taste, religion, and social activities. The American woman was expected to endorse, teach, and uphold a code of behavior that included purity, piety, and propriety. By the 1880s, women virtually dominated the cultural life of the nation. Men were too busy making and losing money and left the gentler aspects of life to their wives.

The popular-song composers recognized and reflected the advancing female culture. Generally eschewing cleverness and satire, the songs dripped with overblown paeans to home, mother, childhood, loss, mourning, and every aspect of nature. Songs like "A Little Faded Rosebud in Our Bible" and "A Flower from My Angel Mother's Grave" managed to successfully combine, commercially if not artistically, all of the themes so appealing to Victorian tastes and hearts.

> *Treasured in my memory like a happy dream,*
> *Are the loving words she gave.*
> *And my heart fondly cleaves*
> *To the dry and withered leaves—*
> *'Tis a flower from my angel mother's grave.*

Home was idealized as the nurturing cocoon in which good habits and behavior were instilled in society's future members. It stood as a beacon of stability, an oasis of safety, peace, and virtue, a sanctuary from the cruel world. This assumption was reflected in such songs as "Dreaming of Home and Mother" by John P. Ordway (1868); "What Is Home Without a

A sentimental love song with an especially beautiful engraved cover (1869).

Mother," written in 1850 by Septimus Winner but popular later; the lovely and still popular "I'll Take You Home Again, Kathleen," written in 1875 by Thomas P. Westendorf; "Driven from Home" (1860) by "Will" Hays; and "Write Me a Letter from Home," written in 1866 by the same author. "Say Will You Ever Return" lamented:

> *If my tears and my prayers can bring you*
> *From far off foreign shore,*
> *Oh bring back my boy,*
> *My pride and my joy,*
> *To your home and your mother once more.*

These and others like them were played on the parlor piano in a miniuniverse of culture of which music was a central element.

The nineteenth-century exaltation of childhood portrayed children as gentle, innocent beings with angelic natures, and songs of the time reflected this belief. The fact that children of Victorian homes were often indulged, spoiled, and rendered unmanageable by passive, fearful mothers and absent, distant fathers was ignored by the songsters. What remains, there-

The popular theater hit song that told young women a story of how purity pays.

Right: A typical book for evenings around the parlor piano.

Turn-of-the-century audiences were eager to buy the music and hear the sad tale of the heroine who dies of a broken heart on the church steps after the "cad" has deserted her (1898). *Collection of Wayland Bunnell*

The death of an innocent little child whose mother bids farewell is dramatically portrayed on this striking cover (1868).

Victorian families idolized their children and idealized childhood. These "little darlings" grace a cover from 1866.

PARLOR SONGS

PRICE
FIFTY
CENTS

fore, is a saccharine presentation of childhood that could only have existed in a grandmother's most indulgent fantasy. Music covers of the time featured roseate-faced, plump-cheeked, docile darlings, arranged prettily on mother's knee—or father's, as mother played the parlor piano.

"Birdie in Heaven" refers to a child with

> Thy bright and golden hair
> The curls thy mother used to twine above thy
>   forehead fair.
> Thy sweet mild eyes so full of love. . . .

And in "Papa, What Would You Take for Me?" a father tells,

> She was ready for sleep and she laid in my arms
> In her little frilled cap so fine.
> With her golden curls peeping out from its edge
> Like a circle of bright sunshine. . . .
> When she sleepily said as she closed her blue eyes,
> "Papa, what would you take for me?"

If children were adored, mothers were elevated to sainthood. They were expected to be fountains of inspiration and models of purity, acting as foils for the world's coarse, aggressive behavior. Saintly martyrdom was not too much to expect, and an aura of spiritual beauty was admired. Motherhood was woman's mission and raison d'être, and popular songs of the period reflected this belief.

Among the broad sphere of Victorian women's responsibilities were those related to death and dying. Lack of medical and general health knowledge resulted in frequent illness and death, and people sickened and died at home. Major epidemics of cholera, typhoid, diphtheria, and measles were common. Images of heaven as an "ideal society" and the dead as "sleeping" were manifested in many songs of the period. The emotions stirred by the songs evoked real tears in their time. Songs such as "Empty Is the Cradle, Baby's Gone," with its chorus,

> Baby left her cradle,
> For the golden shore,
> O'er the silvery waters she has flown.
> Gone to join the angels,
> Peaceful evermore;
> Empty is the cradle, baby's gone,

as well as "Why Did They Dig Ma's Grave So Deep?" "Grandfather's Clock," and "Don't Be Sorrowful, Darling" were popular tearjerkers of their time. Dr. Addison D. Crabtre's "Only a Tramp" (1877) mourns the death of a "nobody" whose silent form the crowd spurns, by reminding them that he

> was somebody's darling, Somebody's son,
> For once he was fair; Once he was young,
> Yes someone has rocked him a baby to sleep,
> Now only a tramp
> Found dead in the street.

Charles A. White and A. G. Chase's "Father Pray With Me Tonight" tells of a little girl whose mother has died, who asks her father,

> Do not turn your head, dear father;
> Try to check that falling tear;
> I mean not to touch your feelings
> When I spoke of mother dear.
> Ah, I miss her too, dear father,
> As I lay me down each night;
> But I know that she is happy
> In that land that's ever bright.

Love songs, of course, were plentiful. Romanticized love, unrequited love, old love, new love, faraway love—all were sung about. "The Day When You'll Forget Me" cries,

> I do not fear the darkest way
> With those dear arms around me;
> Oh no, I only dread the day
> When you can live without me.

Other popular love songs included "White Wings" by Banks Winter; "I'll Meet Her When the Sun Goes Down"; "Treat My Daughter Kindly"; the perennially loved "Silver Threads Among the Gold" by H. P. Danks; Henry Tucker and George Cooper's "Sweet Genevieve," whose sliding chromatic notes make it an eternally favorite barbershop number; "We Parted by the River Side"; and E. N. Catlin's "Love Among the Roses," which chorused:

> She was sitting in the garden,
> Where the little butterfly reposes,
> And how we met, I'll ne'er forget,
> Twas love among the Roses.

Two popular love songs of this period deserve mention for the fact that they were imports from England, a by now unusual occurrence as America had long since been producing its own popular song hits. "When You and I Were Young, Maggie," by James A. Butterfield, and Annie Fortesque Harrison's "In the Gloaming" became part of America's song tradition.

And what happened if the rigid expectations and roles of men and women were spurned, whether by choice or fate? Not everyone, after all, could or would

This song encouraged people to remember that even the tramp on the street was once somebody's baby.

This little girl's heart was broken by her mother's death (1871). Though often overly sentimental, such themes gave cover lithographers, artists, and engravers a chance to show their skill.

abide by the strict Victorian notions of place and propriety, and as the double standard was a firmly held social convention, women who didn't fit the mold were considered to be "fallen angels" and "damaged merchandise." The good girl gone wrong was a highly popular theme of music composers of the late Victorian period. "Mother Was a Lady (If Jack Were Only Here)" concerns the sister who comes to look for her brother Jack in the city. While working as a waitress, she is suggestively insulted by a patron. She begins to cry, and the patron, learning that her brother is his friend and put to shame by her virtue, proposes marriage on the spot. The message was clear, in this and other songs of its ilk: Purity pays. Other songs that dealt with the "fallen" woman included "The Prodigal Daughter's Return," in which an adventurous girl who dallies with her lothario returns home to find her whole family dead of grief; "Take Back Your Gold"; "She Is More to Be Pitied Than Censured"; "Take Her Back, Dad"; and "Without a Wedding Ring," in which the young girl is deserted not only by her beloved who won't marry her, but also by her family who won't forgive her for running away with her lover.

A "fallen angel" song that sold countless copies in

the 1890s was "The Picture That Is Turned Toward the Wall" by Charles Graham, based on the melodrama *Blue Jeans*, about a farmer whose daughter has run away from home. The song chorused:

> There's a name that's never spoken,
> And a mother's heart is broken,
> There is just another missing from the old home,
>   that is all.
> There is still a memory living,
> There's a father unforgiving,
> And a picture that is turned toward the wall.

Although we sometimes laugh at Victorian music now, in its exaggerated pathos and unrelenting sentimentality, it was not funny to its purchasers and players. Each gender's severely proscribed spheres of influence allowed freedom only within acceptable boundaries. Until men and women questioned these unrealistic roles after the turn of the century, music reflected and enhanced them, giving everyone a vision—false though it may have been—of stability and truth in a world trembling frighteningly on the brink of modern times.

Ralph S Weeden

IN THE SHADE
OF THE
OLD APPLE TREE

STELLA BEARDSLY

WORDS
BY
HARRY
WILLIAMS

MUSIC
BY
EGBERT
Van ALSTYNE

Published by
JEROME H. REMICK
AND COMPANY
The Big Firm
Proprietors of
The WHITNEY WARNER PUB. CO.
10 Witherell St., Detroit, Mich. 45 W 28th St. N.Y. 87-89 Clark St., Chicago, Ill.

"HAS ANYBODY HERE SEEN KELLY?"

The Gay Nineties and Beyond

"I Feel a Song Coming On"

TIN PAN ALLEY

Tin Pan Alley—its very name shouts of the brash vitality that characterized it. More than just a place, a group of people, or a few publishing firms, Tin Pan Alley was a way of life in American popular music, with a personality all its own. This personality was to have a revolutionary impact on the popular music business that caused far-reaching reverberations. Although many of its original names and places are now dusty memories, Tin Pan Alley's spirit lives on in its history, methods, songs, and songwriters, as well as in the charming and accurate reflection of American life and tastes during these more innocent times.

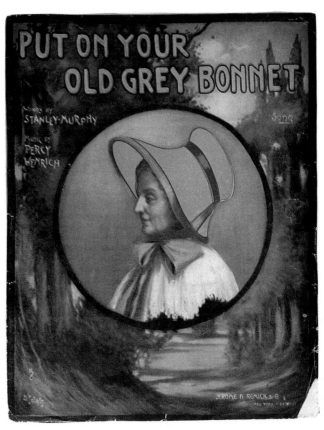

Before 1880, the song publishing industry was fairly disorganized and low key. Major houses were located in various cities and enjoyed similar importance —although Oliver Ditson of Boston possessed the largest catalog of music. However, Root & Cady in Chicago as well as Carl Fischer and G. Schirmer in New York, among others, did a substantial business. If a popular song became a hit, it was purely accidental since there was no universal method of truly aggressive promotion. Dignity prevailed in abundance. Catalogs were issued, and publishers stocked all kinds of music rather than specializing in, say, popular songs or instrumental ar-

Left: A perennial favorite from 1905.

A popular 1909 Tin Pan Alley song with a striking cover, *above,* by Andre DeTakacs.

Tin Pan Alley as it looked in 1914. *Culver Pictures*

rangements. The industry was a refined and genteel one which proudly served its customers and quietly displayed its wares. However, change was on the way.

Sometime in the 1880s, a number of interesting individuals began laying the groundwork for the Tin Pan Alley phenomenon. In 1879, Frank Harding assumed responsibility for his family's publishing firm on New York's Bowery. He began specializing in the publication of popular songs. Eventually, his office became a meeting center for composers and lyricists. Harding was among the first to realize that these individuals needed to be nurtured in a special haven of their own. His firm produced such hits as "My Sweetheart's the Man in the Moon" and "Throw Him Down, McClosky."

In 1881, T. B. Harms set up shop in New York and published "Wait Till the Clouds Roll By," a most successful song. Harms was to practice some innovative marketing methods that heavily influenced the new music business. He cultivated composers from the musical theater and in 1892 was publisher of "The Bowery," a hit from *A Trip to Chinatown*.

In the meantime, a young man in Milwaukee by the name of Charles K. Harris was busy writing "songs to order" for all occasions. Some call this the first real sign of the developing Tin Pan Alley philosophy—aggressively catering to the tastes of the public in

song. He looked to stories, snatches of conversation, and other bits of "real life" for his material. Harris was already sowing seeds that were to grow into Tin Pan Alley's techniques, including persuasively meeting and greeting prospective performers of his works. In 1892, after overhearing a young couple quarrel and separate at a dance in Chicago, he wrote the famous song "After the Ball." It was interpolated into the then popular *A Trip to Chinatown* and sung by J. Aldrich Libby—after some good public relations work by the songwriter. Harris shrewdly assessed the song's potential appeal and, after turning down a lucrative offer from the Witmarks, decided to publish it himself. It was a phenomenal success, escalating to sales of $25,000 per week and ultimately selling 5 million copies. Harris soon opened a publishing firm in New York and continued to enjoy success. He was a major innovator in Tin Pan Alley.

The Witmark brothers began their publishing business on a toy printing press in 1886 in their home on West 40th Street in New York City. They began with "President Grover Cleveland's Wedding March," looking to current events for their theme. Written by Isidore Witmark, it gained enough momentum in the ensuing years to enable the brothers to open a separate office on Union Square. Theirs became a name readily associated with Tin Pan Alley and the music publishing industry for years to come.

E. B. Marks had a curiosity about the entertainment world and a knack for writing lyrics. It was not long before he and Joseph Stern became partners in yet another publishing business generated by a successful song, their sentimental "The Little Lost Child."

The founders of these and other firms were not necessarily trained musicians. Most could not read or write music at all. They hummed melodies to someone else to notate and then penned suitable lyrics. Many were originally salesmen, though, not of music but of such things as buttons, neckties, or corsets. However, their unique sales abilities, recognition of the public's interests, and knack for creating a song put them on the ground floor of Tin Pan Alley.

By the mid-1890s, Union Square was the predominant entertainment center in New York. The minstrel show had faded and was being replaced by variety and vaudeville shows. The area boasted such famous theaters as Tony Pastor's Music Hall, Union Square Theatre, the National Theatre, Miner's Bowery, and the Atlantic Gardens, among others. Songwriters, who had previously been paid a mere $10 or $15 for the outright purchase of songs, only to see the real money pour into the publishers' pockets, became publishers themselves—for example, Harris, the Witmarks, and E. B. Marks. Their establishments were far from elaborate—tiny rooms with rented pianos, and shoestring budgets. Yet their formula for success set them apart. No hit-or-miss sensations for these firms; they made their own hits. Although a variety of songs appealed to their public, the sentimental ballad initially topped the list. Songs of innocent fun and love also sold. Songwriters/publishers studied the current hits and brought out new ones. In addition to "After the Ball," sentimental/fun songs of the era included "Sweet Adeline," "Little Lost Child," and "The Sidewalks of New York."

This was a gilded age in which emotions, even sad ones, were gentler and more innocent. People treasured romance, love, and lighthearted fun. And when their songs were tearjerkers, they favored a good cry, too. Life now was beginning to be more prosperous; civil war was behind and world war not yet truly impending. The country adored singing, dancing, and simpler pleasures, and Tin Pan Alley was more than willing to provide it with songs for every occasion.

Union Square also saw the popularity of a number of "rough-and-tumble" songs, such as "Down Went McGinty" and "Throw Him Down, McClosky," as well as new "coon" songs through which ragtime invaded the Alley.

Songwriters/publishers controlled the style of songs, carefully analyzing what would go over well. Charles K. Harris not only codified a set of guidelines for popular songs of his day, he even published a book called *How to Write a Popular Song*. He knew that the public wanted something familiar or a new song in a familiar style. In his autobiography, he offered such advice as to watch competitors; avoid slang, vulgarity, and multisyllabism; and to include concise lyrics, a strong theme, and a simple melody.

The chorus of the songs became increasingly important and memorable and could often stand alone without the verses. Waltz rhythms and simple major tonal structures were most often used. Romance, happiness, comedy—as in "A Lemon in the Garden of Love" (1906), and sentiment/tragedy prevailed as themes. A specialist in the latter category was Paul Dresser, whose own life was rather sentimentally tragic. His publishing firm was not a business success, although his songs, such as "On the Banks of the Wabash," were popular.

Songwriters read the newspapers avidly for new themes and responded readily to changes in society and the economy, hoping to gain speedy response from the public through topical songs.

The public did not have to come to these firms or rely on catalogs alone to keep abreast of new releases. Publishers went out and introduced their songs through a systematic formula that was at the heart of Tin Pan Alley. Publishers became their own "pluggers." A plugger—originally a "boomer"—was a combined advance man, advertising czar, con artist, and entertainer. Julie Witmark, E. B. Marks, Charles K. Harris, and Joseph Stern, among others, led a colorful life. In addition to their songwriting and publishing activities, they went from variety house to theater to restaurant to burlesque show, bribing orchestras with drinks, greeting performers, giving out free song sheets, offering singers a percentage of profits on sheet-music sales, promising star pictures on sheet-music covers, and standing up and singing an extra chorus when their own song was on the bill. All this was to get their songs played more frequently, interpolated into shows, hummed by the public, and, ultimately, skyrocketed to hits through the sale of large quantities of sheet music. Pluggers often visited a half-dozen establishments on a given evening, turning on their special brand of personal charm.

A number of songwriters for Broadway shows—

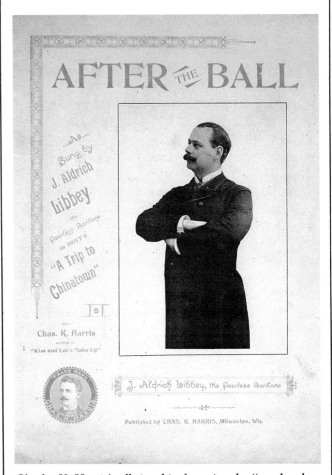

Charles K. Harris's all-time hit, featuring the "peerless baritone," J. Aldrich Libbey (1892).

A sentimental depiction of "love gone wrong" by the prolific Charles K. Harris, whose portrait is on the first page of the music (1908).

Far right: By the prolific team of Andrew B. Sterling and Harry von Tilzer, a song that has been kept alive through oral tradition until today.

Right: Popularized by Nora Bayes, this 1909 song was featured in the musical revue *The Jolly Bachelors*.

HARRY VON TILZER'S GREAT NOVELTY MARCH SONG

WAIT 'TILL THE SUN SHINES, NELLIE

WORDS BY
ANDREW B. STERLING
MUSIC BY
HARRY VON TILZER

Gladys Fisher

JENKINS

HARRY VON TILZER
MUSIC PUBLISHING CO.
37 W 28 St NEW YORK. CHICAGO. FRISCO. LONDON

5

Victor Herbert, George M. Cohan, Rudolf Friml—became favorite names on Tin Pan Alley. If the show was a success, sales of sheet music—often available for purchase in the lobby after the performance—would soar. These composers were on the top of the list for "nurturing" by publishing firms.

Around the turn of the century, publishers began making their way a little farther uptown to 28th Street between Fifth and Sixth avenues. The old Union Square crowd emigrated here along with some new faces such as Leo Feist, Harry von Tilzer, and Gus Edwards. Here the business really came into its own. The song plugger blossomed into an incredibly important figure. Sales in excess of one million, a rarity in Union Square, became frequent on 28th Street. Between 1900 and 1910, more than one hundred songs sold more than a million copies. "Let Me Call You Sweetheart" (1910) sold 8 million. Many of these songs passed to oral tradition and are still familiar, loved, and sung today.

The output of Tin Pan Alley between 1890 and 1910 also reflected the true spirit of the gilded age. "The Band Played On," "When You Were Sweet Sixteen," "In the Good Old Summertime," and "Sweet Rosie O'Grady" are just a few examples from this romantic, sentimental era. The population and the economy had expanded and the public was ready to enjoy and to buy the songs. By 1900, only a few songs were published outside of New York. Those of Carrie Jacobs Bond and Will Rossiter were notable and longstanding exceptions.

It was on 28th Street that Tin Pan Alley was actually given its name. There are several versions of the story, but all seem to agree that Monroe Rosenfeld—newspaperman, composer, gambler, and general character-around-town—played a key role. One version holds that when Rosenfeld was interviewing Harry von Tilzer for an article about the music business, he noticed that von Tilzer's piano had been stuffed with paper to produce a tinny sound. In the article, which he titled "Tin Pan Alley," Rosenfeld said the sound of this and other pianos pounding through the open windows resembled tin pans being clashed together. The name stuck, and Tin Pan Alley soon came to mean the song business and the song style it popularized. Von Tilzer, incidentally, turned out such hits as "A Bird in a Gilded Cage," "Wait Till the Sun Shines, Nellie," and "I Want a Girl."

Many famous names were once pluggers and staff songwriters on Tin Pan Alley—George Gershwin, Jerome Kern, and Irving Berlin among them. Eventually, they would experiment with new harmonic, rhythmic, and melodic concepts that took Tin Pan Alley away from the tried-and-true clichés of Harris and Marks and gave its products new sophistication and deeper beauty.

World War I saw the production of an abundance of songs, tied into social events, war episodes, and sentiments of the time. This has often been called the heyday of Tin Pan Alley. Sheet music was produced in huge quantities, and sold quickly as the public responded to the event-linked themes and covers. As the world became increasingly embroiled in conflict, however, the emotions of the gilded age were joined by more somber and complex ones, and song content responded in kind.

In addition to increasing the sophistication of popular music and expanding its production, the Alley became the source of another improvement—protection of its composers. Until World War I, the composer's income was derived from the sale of sheet music alone. Whereas a solo artist or an orchestra gained fame and popularity from performing a certain song, the songwriter received no compensation. This thought struck Victor Herbert one evening while he was listening to the orchestra at Shanley's on 43rd Street play one of his selections. He concluded that some sort of organization was needed to protect composers' interests. Herbert called together a number of interested individuals at Luchow's restaurant and they conceived of a plan that eventually led to the formation of the American Society of Composers, Authors & Publishers (ASCAP). It took several years and some court decisions to make ASCAP a practical organization, but ultimately it succeeded. An establishment that used music for "public consumption" now needed a license to use a work of an ASCAP member, and had to pay a fee or a royalty for this use. By 1921, ASCAP members began to draw royalties from clubs, theaters, radio, and records.

Originally, composers were given an arbitrary rating that determined the income that they would receive. For example, "name" composers like Kern, Gershwin, Cole Porter, and Richard Rodgers were given an AA rating. However, this system ultimately became one that was based on the number of performances of a work or works, a more equitable method. Broadcast Music Inc. (BMI) was a similar organization that acted to protect the rights of its members, and engaged in fierce struggles with ASCAP over radio networks in 1941, before reaching a mutual agreement over respective rights and territories.

After World War I, Tin Pan Alley changed form. Many of the offices began moving up into the West 40s near the theater district, and certain places such as the Brill Building and Radio City ultimately became the latter-day centers of the Alley. But it was not the same. The world was changing, and so was the world of music publishing. With the advent of the recording industry, jukeboxes, radio, and "talkies," promoting a song became a more elaborate process. There were more and varied customers to visit and more complicated procedures to follow. By 1930, the days of the plugger winning the loyalty of the variety star to promote a hit song were but an echo, and 28th Street was a ghostly memory. Many of the old firms were bought out by large corporations—Warner took over Witmark, Harms, and Remick—seeking huge profits in Hollywood. Unlike the pioneering entrepreneurs with a song in their heads and a new opportunity to plug ever waiting, composers were now solely musically oriented songwriters who left the business aspects of music publishing to others.

Tin Pan Alley was gone, replaced by a nationwide industry of incredible sophistication. Yet when the strains of "After the Ball," "The Bowery," or innumerable other melodies are heard, one cannot help but remember the Alley—its heroes, its rogues, its charm, and its hits. Here lay the groundwork for the American popular music business as we know it today.

"Ragging the Scale"

RAGTIME

RAGTIME CRIED OUT TO BE THE NEXT WAVE of popular music in America. Surfeited by sentiment yet bound inextricably by the mores of the fading Victorian Age, Americans were ripe for something new.

A stepchild of the "coon" song and of the cakewalk —which started a dance craze—of the late 1800s, ragtime captured the imagination of the public in unprecedented numbers. The coon song had been very popular, and remained so in theater and vaudeville through the first decade of the twentieth century with such hits as "Hush, My Little Coon," "My Pickaninny Babe," "Every Race Has a Flag But the Coon," and "I'll Eat Watermelon Till I Die." Yet the racial stereotyping and crude portrayal of blacks guaranteed its eventual demise. The lively, rhythmic music of the songs must surely have influenced the creators of ragtime, although as late as the 1880s, it had yet to be identified as a unique form.

The cakewalk craze was precipitated by Kerry Mills, writer of "At a Georgia Camp Meeting" (1897) and "Rastus on Parade" (1895). The terms *ragtime* and *cakewalk* were often used interchangeably by the music industry and the public in the first years of the ragtime craze.

Ragtime is basically a written piano music. Its rhythm is marchlike 2/4 time, played steadily by the left hand, while the top melody line is set against the bass line in a syncopation created by a note delayed or advanced by half a beat. The stress falls unexpectedly between beats. As Eubie Blake once said, "Anything that is syncopated is basically ragtime. I don't

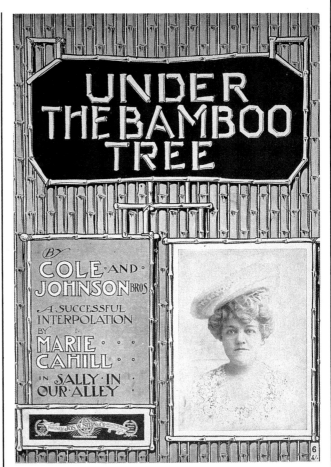

Interpolated into *Sally in Our Alley,* this song by Cole and Johnson has an exotic locale and used syllabification to intensify the ragtime effect.

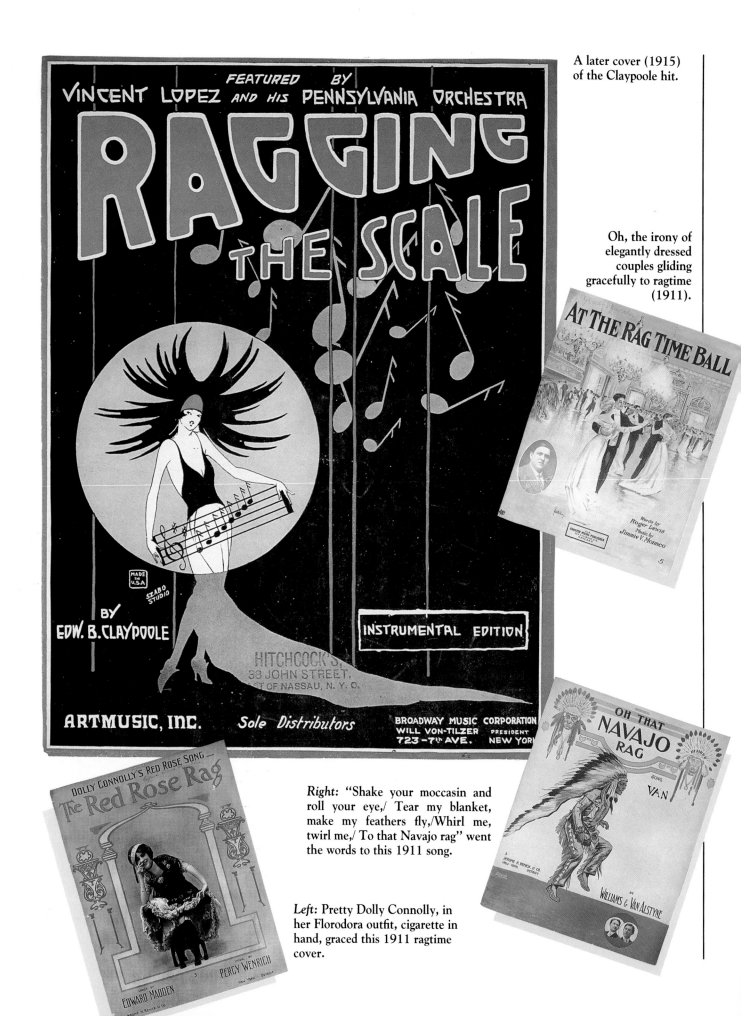

A later cover (1915) of the Claypoole hit.

Oh, the irony of elegantly dressed couples gliding gracefully to ragtime (1911).

Right: "Shake your moccasin and roll your eye,/ Tear my blanket, make my feathers fly,/Whirl me, twirl me,/ To that Navajo rag" went the words to this 1911 song.

Left: Pretty Dolly Connolly, in her Florodora outfit, cigarette in hand, graced this 1911 ragtime cover.

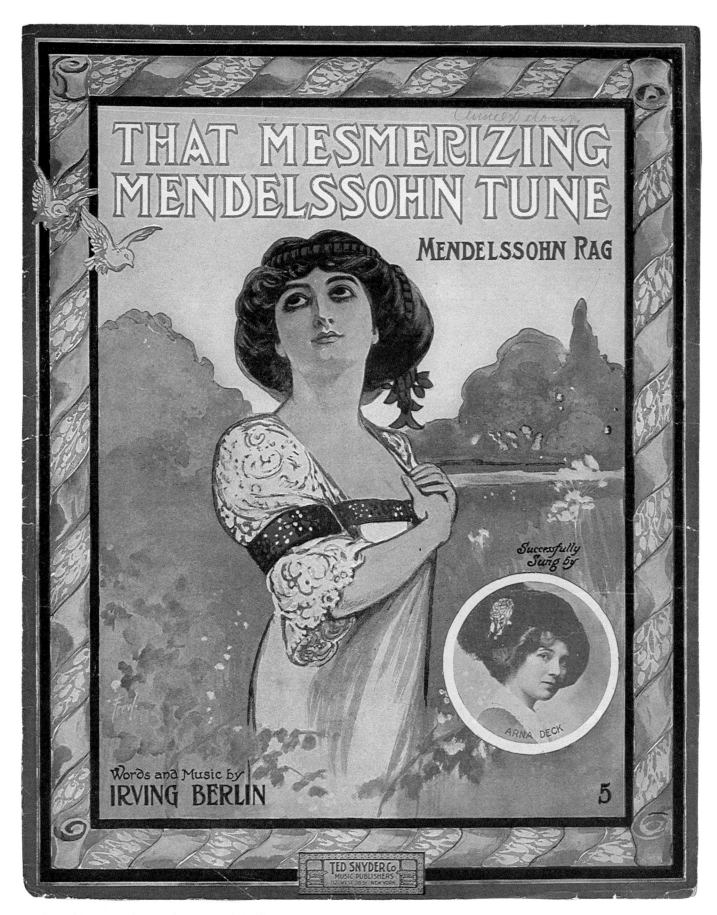

One of Irving Berlin's earliest songs (1909).

care whether it's Liszt's 'Hungarian Rhapsody' or Tchaikovsky['s] 'Waltz of the Flowers.' "

It was this syncopation, this rhythm that captured the ear and heart of a public sick of mediocrity and gloom and that soon had nearly everyone "living a ragtime life."

In its purest forms, ragtime was an instrumental music. Most of its early fame came via the piano and through its many fine pianistic interpreters, such as Jesse Pickett, Otis Saunders, and Ben Harney.

The American public discovered ragtime at the 1893 Chicago World's Fair. Three years later the singer and pianist Ben Harney appeared at Tony Pastor's 14th Street Theatre in New York City and made a reputation for himself as "The Inventor of Ragtime." His impact was dynamic.

The first ragtime compositions were published in 1897. They included "Louisiana Rag" by Theodore H. Northrup and "Mississippi Rag" by William H. Krell. Others followed that same year and included Tom Turpin's "Harlem Rag" (Chicago) and Paul Sarebresole's "Roustabout Rag" (New Orleans). By the end of the century, the word *ragtime* was used to sell all manner of sheet music published in major cities throughout the United States. The music was hot, and publishers scrambled to catch the bandwagon. Until 1907, ragtime popularity gathered momentum. From 1908 until World War I, it engendered a music boom that often precipitated loose interpretations and dilution of the purity of its original form. No matter —the public bought it all. Soon, Tin Pan Alley was creating "ragtime songs," a contradiction in terms. As a category, ragtime was eventually to become somewhat eclectic. There were pure rags, modified rags, and parodies of rags. Ted Snyder's "Wild Cherries Rag" (1908), Irving Berlin's "That Mesmerizing Mendelssohn Tune" (1909)—an example of "ragging" the classics—and Percy Wenrich's "Red Rose Rag" (1911) enjoyed enormous success.

Ragtime, which had largely been a music of black culture and performers, rapidly caught on in white circles, with women especially. Female creators of ragtime included the well-known May Aufderheide— "Dusty Rag" and "Buzzer Rag"; Adaline Shepherd— "Pickles and Peppers"; and Sadie Koninsky. The result was a modified rag that caught on quickly, especially when Tin Pan Alley realized that publishing ragtime was a surefire way to please the public and to make money. "Rag Bag Rag," "Waiting for the Robert E. Lee," and "Alexander's Ragtime Band" are just a few of the rags that became popular hits in the modified rag category.

All-black vaudeville and theatrical shows with rag-time, such as *Clorindy*, also catered to the passion for the new form. By the time the "Galli-Curci Rag" appeared in *The Passing Show of 1918*, ragtime was commonly incorporated into "white" productions.

By 1911, even European classical composers such as Claude Debussy were writing "raggy" music. The American Scott Joplin had already written "Maple Leaf Rag" (1899), supposedly the first instrumental sheet music to sell one million copies. Although this figure is in dispute, it still reflects the immense popularity of the composition and of the genre. Other Joplin works included "Swipsy" (1900), "Peacherine Rag" (1901), "The Easy Winners" (1901), "The Entertainer" (1902), "Weeping Willow" (1903), and "The Cascades" (1904).

Joplin was considered to be a "serious" ragtime composer whose rags took a good degree of pianistic skill to perform. From an itinerant piano player and composer, he came to be known as the King of Ragtime through his compositions. He also tried his hand at an opera, "Treemonisha," which incorporated ragtime into its score.

Other rags of the "classical" style included Charles Johnson's "Porcupine Rag" (1909), James Scott's "Hilarity Rag" (1909), Egbert Van Alstyne's "Easy Pickin's" (1902), Bob Coles's "Under the Bamboo Tree" (1902), and Tom Turpin's "St. Louis Rag" (1903).

Despite the popularity of "Maple Leaf Rag" and Joplin's and other composers' devotion to the pure form of the art, a more boisterous type of ragtime was spreading. Some segments of society viewed this music as evil and suggestive. Whether or not this reaction stemmed from ragtime's lively syncopations, its performance in cabarets, saloons, and brothels did much to spread its reputation as a corrupting influence.

Ben Harney produced exuberant rags of this type. Many of his compositions had words, and were sung not only by himself but also by "coon shouters" at various places of entertainment. Harney's "Mr. Johnson Turn Me Loose" always brought down the house.

As thousands of rags followed, sheet-music cover art burst into its grandest experimentation yet. Most notable were the use of color and design and the development of Art Nouveau, early Cubist, and Art Deco themes.

Ragtime never really died. It lives on in jazz, swing, and rock-and-roll. Its echoes excite us today; its merry tunes and bright rhythms live on in our piano benches as masterpieces of popular art—beautifully colored sheets and a truly American music.

This wonderfully creative and humorous ragtime cover is by Andre DeTakacs.

This title features a clever play on words (1912).

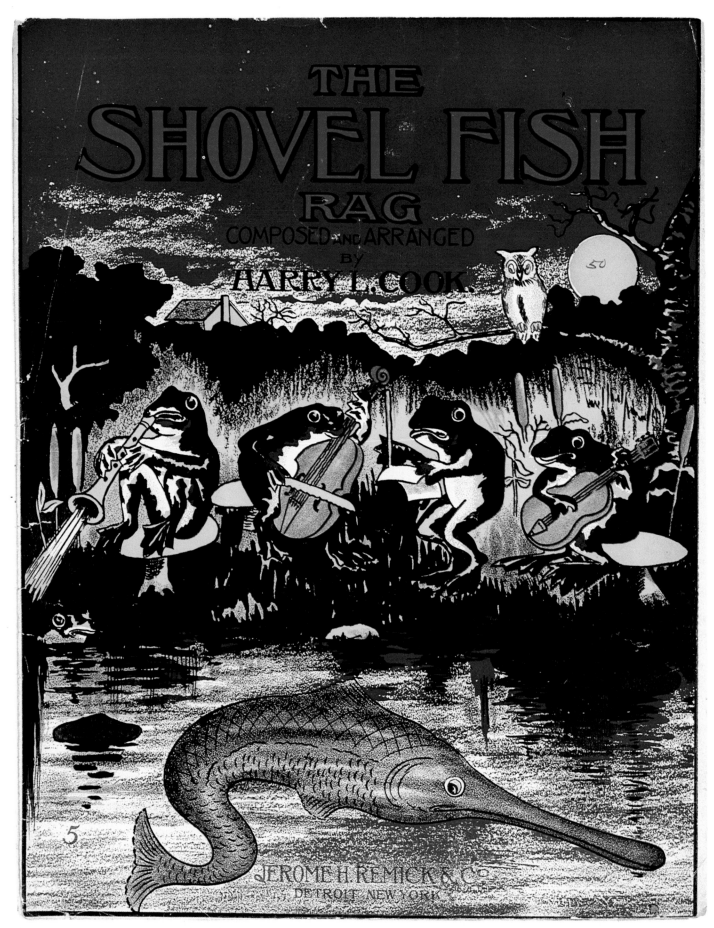

A less-seen 1908 rag with an extremely colorful and comic cover.

"The Castle Waltz"

THE DANCE CRAZE

THE TEMPO OF AMERICAN LIFE WAS picking up with amazing speed, the result of the popularization of inventions such as the automobile, airplane, and motion picture. America's horizons were broadening and its capacity for experimentation was widening. As always, popular music reflected these changes.

Between 1910 and 1920, American popular music *was* dance. It wasn't enough to be able to hum along or sing the chorus, you had to be able to dance to it too. And dance we did, to some of the most inventive

—and short-lived—jiggles and jumps, dips and dives, that music and dance history have ever known.

The dance craze came in on the coattails of ragtime. For many years, Americans had been extremely stilted on the dance floor. Strict propriety had demanded the old-fashioned waltz. Even in the public dance halls and beer gardens, and especially the ballrooms, the old quadrilles and reels had been set aside only for the modest two-step.

Ragtime changed everything. The cakewalk, with

A dance cover that used black stereotypes of the time (1917).

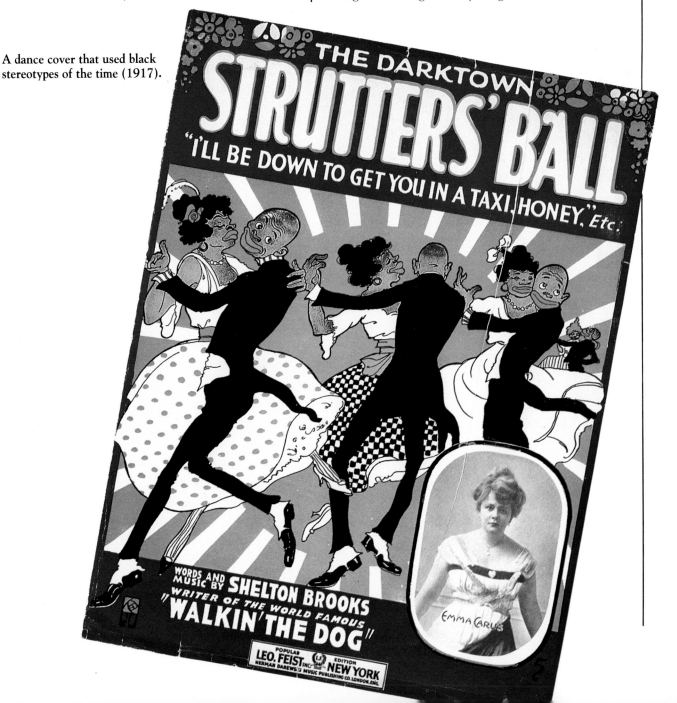

Vernon and Irene Castle in 1913. *Bettmann Archive*

became the rage. From 1912 through 1914, more than a hundred new dances were adopted. Tin Pan Alley cranked out thousands of tunes which, although they sometimes contained lyrics, were always danceable and set to orchestrations for dancing.

New rhythmic structures led to more complex steps, and new attitudes led to more sensuous intimacy while dancing. Newspapers raged that these dances were "demoralizing the young" and were responsible for the "deterioration of manners." Churches condemned them, judges pronounced fines, and everyone was dancing them. It was estimated that half a million people in New York were part of the "dancing set."

The fox-trot became an appealing attraction. "My Fox-Trot Girl," "The Jelly Roll Blues," and "Ballin' the Jack" were among the numerous songs that served to spark the country into dancing this catchy step.

Animal imitations headed the list of fox-trot variations. Such innovations as the Turkey Trot, Bunny Hug, Chicken Scratch, Kangaroo Dip, Possom Trot, and Grizzly Bear prevailed. The latter helped to accelerate the spread of the dance craze. The 1910 song of the same title, by Berlin and Botsford, initiated a dance whereby the partners hugged each other and rocked from side to side in time to the music. The sheet music featured the ever-popular Sophie Tucker on the cover.

The waltz was not forgotten—just modified into the Hesitation. "Daddy Long Legs," "Illusion," and "One Wonderful Night" were among the popular titles in this category.

More dances took hold. From the One-Step, Two-Step, the Texas Tommy, the Snake, the Crab Step, to the Airplane Dip, America was on its feet and moving.

The dance craze reached its undeniable height with the popularity of the great dance team of Vernon and Irene Castle. Although they nearly starved at the outset of their career, their European success brought them solid assurance of a warm acceptance upon returning to America. The Castles and other ballroom dance teams, such as Maurice and Walton, were extremely graceful and skillful in their execution of scores of new and catchy dances. The public loved to watch them and imitate them, and hungrily purchased the music that they danced to.

The Castles fed the country's growing interest in the new and exotic. They introduced a number of Latin dances—the South American tango and the Cuban rhumba, the conga, the samba, and the Brazilian maxixe. The team also created dances of their own, such as the Castle Walk, a variation of the

tunes like "Golliwogs Cake Walk" and "Sambo Outa Work Cake Walk," brought Afro-American elements into the popular dance repertoire. Spreading from South and West, it was integrated into other dance forms, such as the tango, which encouraged livelier forms of social dancing. Dances that had been seen and done mainly in honky-tonks and bordellos were soon adopted by Eastern middle and upper classes.

The passion for speed, sophistication, and worldly awareness found an outlet in scores of dances that

Toddle. Numerous song titles bore witness to the Castles' popularity. Specially written numbers included "Castle Lame Duck," "Castle House Rag," "Castle Classic Waltz," "Castle Innovation Waltz (Esmeralda)," "Castle Hesitation Waltz," and "Castle Tango."

The business that this fabulous team generated was awe-inspiring. They organized dance schools, orchestras, and nightclubs. Their world-renowned Castle House was a studio, and they also gave exhibitions for society. They initiated a national craze for the *thé dansant,* an afternoon tea—or something stronger—with dancing. The Castles made the new dances a part of high society, therefore respectable. Their popularity soared until Vernon Castle's tragic death during World War I while serving as a pilot in the air force.

The dance craze generated huge sales of records and sheet music. Dance teachers ran brisk businesses in guiding ordinary dancers in the navigation of complicated steps. Orchestras sprang up to ensure live music for hotels and dance halls at teatime and in the evenings.

America's verve, energy, and jaded sophistication was to continue to expand. The dance craze of the teens laid the groundwork for the variety of dances and dance songs to come in the twenties and beyond. It served as a springboard for the country to express itself and experiment with new musical forms. It offered a respite from the depressing statistics of World War I death tolls and helped usher America into yet another and more sophisticated age.

With the rise of dance music, full-time orchestras and dance bands developed from the formerly haphazard method of putting together a few musicians at the last minute. Society audiences demanded good orchestras at the large ballrooms in the better hotels. This was a foretaste of the great, thirty-year-long dance-band era that was to come.

The dance craze was the impetus for some of the most colorful and innovative sheet-music covers ever produced. Covers on sheets such as "Fairy Queen (Intermezzo and Two-Step)," "Tres Moutarde (One or Two-Step or Tango)," and "By Heck (Eccentric Fox Trot)" are a few of thousands with brilliant color and design inspired by the songs of the dance-craze era.

After the Armistice that ended World War I, the nation headed into the Roaring Twenties. America danced then too—the Charleston, the Shimmy, and the Black Bottom, among others—but never again would popular music and dance be one as they were when couples did the "Gaby Glide" while the gunfire at Verdun echoed around the world.

This man must go away and recuperate from overdoing the Hesitation step.

Haselden's famous cover from 1911 gave dance-crazed couples the opportunity to do the one- or two-step or the tango.

Every activity was
grist for the dance mill (1912).

Right: This dancing song features a
fantastic Art Nouveau cover (1908).

The cover of this dance sensation featured a beautiful redhead.

"I'm Glad You're Goin', Goodbye"

SUNDAY SUPPLEMENTS

THERE HAS NEVER BEEN A LACK of creative and innovative ideas in the world of song distribution. It comes as no surprise, therefore, that publishers and promoters, intent upon popularizing a song, composer, or star, seized upon newspapers as an outlet for their efforts as well as store and manufacturing company giveaways.

One can only surmise that the idea of getting something for nothing was more exciting than the music itself proved to be. "Try this over on your piano" may have elicited groans of boredom. In any case, with a few exceptions, it is not the music that caused a very few people to hang on to these sheets, but probably rather their colorful, intriguing covers.

Music sheets were given away in stores of all types as well as by companies themselves and were inserted into newspaper Sunday supplements for the purpose not of selling a product but of popularizing a new song. It is remarkable that any of the newspaper inserts have survived: newsprint yellows and disintegrates very quickly and most people must have considered these sheets the ultimate throwaway. Good copies are therefore considered rare treasures and are much sought-after collector's items.

From approximately 1895 to the 1920s, this sheet music, known as the Sunday Supplement, was in vogue. The song sheet within the weekly news was a free extra for the price of the paper. The reader could try the music at home on the piano and, it was hoped, might be inspired to purchase additional musical numbers. The covers, drawn by regular newspaper artists, were often comical and unusual. Such diverse songs as "There's a Dark Man Coming With a Bundle," with a cover by Swinnerton, the creator of Foxy Grandpa; "Happy Hooligan March & Two-Step"; and "American Girl March" by Victor Herbert were found tucked between the folds of newsprint. Even as late as 1942, the *New York Journal American* presented to its readers what they called the first great song of World War II, "Remember Pearl Harbor."

Additional newspaper supplements included "I Love My Dolly Best" (1898, the *New York Journal*), "My Indian Maiden" (1904, the *New York American and Journal*—illustration by H. B. Eddy), and "I'm Glad You're Goin', Goodbye" (1912, the *New York Tribune*). The last is an example of a sheet printed on high-quality paper instead of newsprint.

Similar to the Sunday Supplement was the advertising song sheet, whose purpose was to market something to the public en masse. Instead of promoting songs, composers, and stars, the advertising sheet promoted a product.

"Wait for the Wagon" was issued by the Studebaker brothers in 1884 and distributed free to customers. Its lyrics, a parody of the original, extol the virtues of the firm's wagon. After that, firms such as the Bromo Seltzer Company (1890), the Cable Piano Company (1903), and others issued songs to advertise their products. Although most of the songs were backed by single advertisers, "Miss Samantha Johnson's Wed-

An 1878 supplement to the *New York Family Story Paper*.

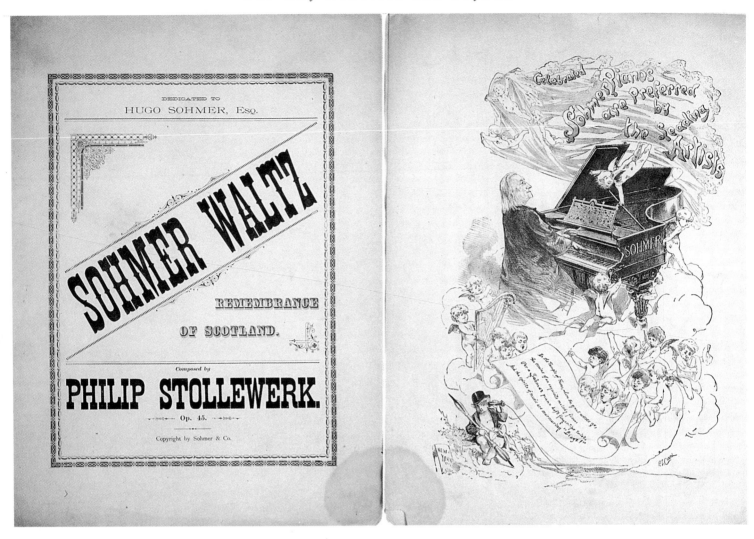

An advertising giveaway that extols the virtues of the Sohmer piano (1887).

ding Day" was stamped by no less than twenty firms —a testament to the great popularity of this marketing medium.

Other advertising sheets include:

"Petroleum Court Dance," 1865; the front cover of the litho shows a giant oil well with the words "New York, Philadelphia and Baltimore Consolidated Petroleum and Mining Co." The back cover contains an offer of the stock and lists names and addresses of the company offices.

"The Fish Bitters," 1868; pictures a fish-shaped patent medicine bottle.

"The Knabe Polka," 1871; a picture of the Knabe factory appears on the back cover.

"The Merry Singer," 1891; Singer sewing machine.

"Regina March," 1895; Regina music boxes.

"Love I Adore You," 1900; musical supplement to the *New York Sunday Press* with words by George Cooper.

"Lucinda, Cinda, Jane," 1901; the Schubert Piano Co., with a black-stereotype cover.

"Honeymoon for Three," 1949; Chevrolet.

Another cousin to the Sunday Supplement and the advertising song sheet is the musical postcard. Particularly popular around the turn of the century, these small oddities had music and illustrations that advertised performers, songs, and movie music via the mail. Even some local color managed to creep in. You could send a greeting with the music to "On Jersey Shore" that depicted a popular bandmaster of the day.

Each of these supplementary music categories is a rare remembrance of yesteryear for the collector and well worth the search for a prime item.

A 1912 supplement to the *New York Tribune, above,* and a supplement to the *New York American and Journal* (1904), featuring a popular chanteuse of the day, *above left.*

Right: Revelers in exotic costume celebrate in an exceptionally fine lithograph by Teller Sons & Dorner, N.Y. (1897).

A rare black collectible, this was an advertising gift from the Schubert Piano Company in 1901.

"The Burning of Rome"

E. T. PAULL

THE NAME E. T. PAULL INSTANTLY conjures up brilliant colors flashing across oversized covers of turn-of-the-century sheet music. It is interesting to note that his contemporaries found the music as attractive as the covers.

Paull's musical ability was enhanced by his skill in mirroring the tastes of the masses and in marketing his output. He published some two hundred marches, gallops, waltzes, trots, and musical novelties, as well as folios and a series of classical music transcriptions. He is best known for his thundering marches, written on practically every conceivable subject, playable by the amateur and with an appeal to a broad range of emotions that could be evoked on one's parlor piano.

Paull was allegedly dubbed The New March King by *The New York Music Trade Review* and *The Music Trades*, leading musical journals of the time. Many of his works represented stirring descriptions of historical events—"The Burning of Rome," "Charge of the Light Brigade," and "Paul Revere's Ride." Others were patriotic—"America Forever March," "Lincoln Centennial March," and "We'll Stand By the Flag March," and still others depicted stirring natural, current, and social scenes—"The Storm King March," "The Dawn of the Century March," "The Circus Parade March and Two-Step," and "N.Y. and Coney Island Cycle March."

Many of these songs contained elaborate written descriptions as an aid to the performer. "The Burning of Rome" carries Paull's page-long "explanatory" of the song, detailing events as they will appear in the music. Little notations such as "Finish of the Race," "Alarm of Fire," and "Crash of Falling Walls" dot the musical text. Although his are not the earliest examples of descriptive marches, he published more of this type than anyone else. The combination of the music and descriptions gives the marches the feel of an accompaniment for a silent movie. In the advance artist copies of some of his later works, the advertisements are directed toward the silent movie industry, and since Paull lived in New York City from 1896 on, there is no doubt that his work from 1900 to 1920 was influenced by the presence there of the fledgling movie industry.

Paull was active as an arranger as well as composer. The famous "Midnight Fire Alarm" was actually composed by Harry J. Lincoln and arranged for piano by E. T. Paull.

Paull loved action, as evidenced by the subjects of his pieces and the writtten notations included in them. His piano arrangements were full of action too —a veritable feast of cascading octaves, sprightly bass lines, and flashy finales. A contemporary description of his work stated: "His compositions give universal satisfaction. All of his marches are wonderfully stirring, bright, catchy, and inspiring throughout. One of the chief characteristics of Mr. Paull's compositions is that they lay well under the fingers and are comparatively easy to play."

Edward T. Paull was born in Gerrardstown, West Virginia, February 16, 1858. He was the son of Henry Washington Paull and Margaret C. Thornburg and had two sisters, Laura May and Mary. Paull's father was a farmer and, later, after a move to Martinsburg, Virginia, a boardinghouse keeper.

At the age of twenty, E. T. Paull was running his own piano and organ business. However, although his father was quite prosperous, it took Paull a while to become so, and his father had to pay off debts incurred during Paull's early business years.

In 1894, Paull's first music copyright, "The Chariot Race" or "Ben Hur March," appeared and was an instant success. He was thirty-six. At this time, he was general manager of the Richmond (Virginia) Music Company, and original copyrights were taken out in the company's name. "The Chariot Race" was followed by "What Might Have Been," "The Della Fox Little Trooper March," and a song entitled "The Old Man's Story," which was changed to "The Stranger's Story" prior to publication. All of them carried the Richmond Music Co. imprint. "The Chariot Race" sold 60,000 copies the first year and continued to sell strongly into the 1920s. Its recording by John Philip Sousa and later connection with the silent film *Ben Hur* helped stimulate sales for a long period. Paull's "Charge of the Light Brigade" was also a successful seller.

Financial security now enabled Paull to embark on a phenomenally lucrative and varied music publishing career. His connection with the Hoen Lithograph Company of Richmond ensured the future popularity of his music. Hoen provided most of the remarkable

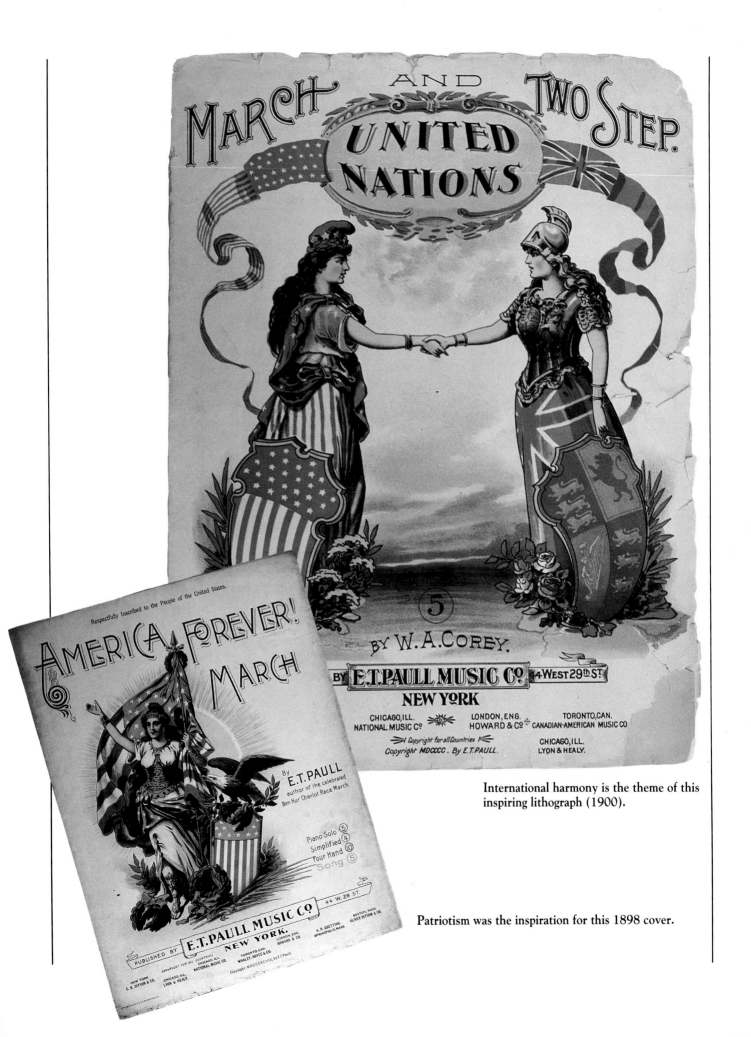

International harmony is the theme of this inspiring lithograph (1900).

Patriotism was the inspiration for this 1898 cover.

America's infatuation with the exotic
inspired this 1901 Hoen lithograph.

A historical event is featured in all its drama
and fury (1903).

A sense of whirling motion created in the music is reflected in a cover of 1901.

A sentimental coon song featuring a "courtin' " couple. Collection of Wayland Bunnell

"Coon" songs carried black stereotypes to their most extreme as shown in a rare cover of 1909. Collection of Wayland Bunnell

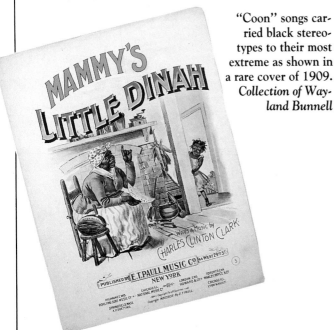

covers, done in an unusual five-color process, which collectors seek so avidly today.

The artist who created these wonderful specimens is, sadly, unknown; they are known merely as E. T. Paull lithos. One advertisement aptly said that these works were "embellished with the Handsomest, most

Striking and Characteristic Title Pages ever seen on Music."

In about April 1896, Paull moved to New York City. His publishing company moved at least five times between 1896 and 1926, which accounts for the different street addresses in the publishing credits at the bottom of the music covers. During this successful period, Paull had increased opportunities to indulge his love of action both in advertisement and, more important, in colorful lithographs. As far as advertising was concerned, who could resist the following appeal to buy one of his latest marches?

NAPOLEON'S LAST CHARGE—March-Gallop.

WRITTEN AND ARRANGED BY E. T. PAULL

This is positively one of the Greatest March Compositions ever written. Mr. Paull spent nearly two years on this piece, to have it the best published. It represents the downfall of Napoleon, the mighty conqueror of Europe, at the Battle of Waterloo. It has been made descriptive throughout, and represents the Bugle Call to Arms, Cavalry Call, Army Marching and Forming Line of Battle, Band Playing and Cannonading; Cavalry Advancing; Horses Galloping; Clash of Arms, Death in the Sunken Trench, etc. Every one who plays or uses music in any way should certainly have a copy of this great piece.

The colorful, action-packed covers of Paull's sheet music were well known and proved to have lasting appeal. The five-color lithos exude movement, liveliness, disaster, tumult, patriotism, and a host of other qualities. Chariots race, horse-drawn fire engines charge through the streets, and whole cities burst into flames as reds, yellows, greens, browns, and blues splash vividly across the page. In fact, if it were not for those gorgeous covers, Paull would have a small, if not practically nonexistent, place in sheet-music history.

Different paper used, resulting in variations of the vivid hues in the covers, reflected work coming out of the different publishing houses. Some were produced on bright white paper; earlier pieces used off-white paper, resulting in more subdued tones. Earlier runs of lithographed covers were often more detailed, whereas later editions appeared somewhat grainy, reflecting wear on the lithographic stones.

The other two major lithographers and cover artists for E. T. Paull were J. E. Rosenthal, whose covers include "By the Lakes of Killarney," "Mammy's Little Dinah," and "Old Church Door," and Bert Cobb, whose titles include "Arizona," "Mandy, Mandy," and "Oh Joe, Dear Joe."

This march was written in honor of General Lew Wallace, author of the hugely successful novel *Ben Hur* (1896).

Another exciting, action-packed E. T. Paull cover (1900).

Paull's music was often dedicated to individuals, groups, or organizations, and many songs had political or military themes. A sizable portion as well were "coon" songs, many published around the turn of the century when racist images were acceptable in entertainment.

Paull published for nearly forty years. Much of the music is in a large-size (11 × 14-inch) format. Postwar pieces will be found in the standard 10 × 12-inch size.

E. T. Paull died on November 25, 1924, and was buried in Evergreen Cemetery, Brooklyn. He left a legacy of work that reflected America's taste at the time and whose cover art remains unmatched in its powerful use of line and color.

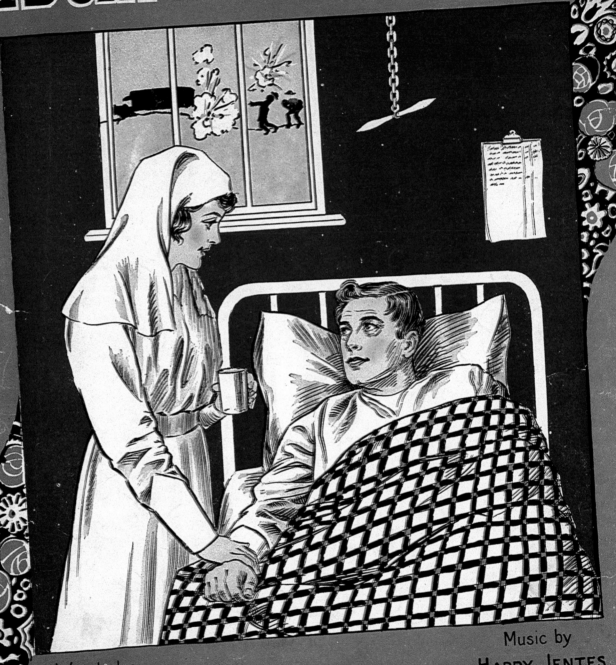

I Don't Want To Get Well

Words by
HARRY PEASE
and
HOWARD JOHNSON

Music by
HARRY JENTES

POPULAR EDITION
LEO. FEIST INC. NEW YORK
HERMAN DAREWSKI MUSIC PUBLISHING CO. LONDON, ENG.

"IN MY MERRY OLDSMOBILE"

Transitions

"Over There"

SONGS OF WORLD WAR I

The shots that rang out in Sarajevo on June 28, 1914, foreshadowed the end of a gracious age and signaled the start of an unspeakable horror—the world at war. As Archduke Francis Ferdinand lost his life to the bullet of a Serbian patriot, so too the world lost an innocence it was never to regain.

Names such as Ypres, Flanders, and Gallipoli were to be etched in the world's mind with the most solemn of memories. Empires tumbled, making way for new nations. Sophisticated weapons of death were introduced—poison gas, tanks, submarines. Ten million were to die and paths of pillage and ruin were the grim rewards of a war that spanned the globe. The world was never to be the same.

Although the United States did not enter the war at its inception, Americans were keenly aware of mounting tensions in Europe and subsequent events on the front. Their interest was demonstrated by the popularity in 1915 of several British soldier songs,

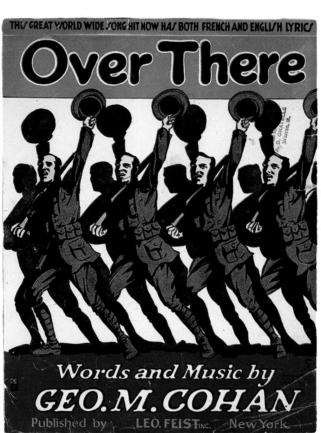

such as "Keep the Home Fires Burning" and "Pack Up Your Troubles in Your Old Kit-Bag and Smile, Smile, Smile."

In 1915, Woodrow Wilson campaigned for president on the slogan "He kept us out of war." Although both Wilson and the country pretended that the United States could stay out of international conflicts and remain isolationist, most songwriters seemed to know better. In the campaign song "Go Right Along, Mr. Wilson," written by A. Seymour Brown and published in 1915 by Jerome H. Remick and Company, it was clear that the songwriter, mirroring the mood of the country, was subtly preparing the nation for war, asking people to ready themselves while at the same time encouraging Wilson to make peace.

Still, Americans, many of them first- or second-

Above: One of many versions of the popular Cohan song.

Left: A tribute to the battlefield angels of mercy.

generation citizens, torn between loyalty to their ancestral country and loyalty to their adopted one, prayed fervently for peace and sang such tunes as "Uncle Sam Won't Go to War" and "We Stand for Peace While Others War." The best-known of the antiwar songs appeared in 1915. Written by Alfred Bryan and Al Piantadosi and titled "I Didn't Raise My Boy to Be a Soldier," it capitalized on people's conflicts about sacrificing their children's lives for a war "over there."

On the other hand, there was a staunch patriotism and willingness to protect home and country. "America, I Love You" and "We'll Never Let Our Flag Fall" exhibit this spirit. "In Time of Peace Prepare for War" shows that Americans were indeed aware of the inevitable course of events.

Increasingly, people's hopes for peace dimmed as the incidents of threats to American shipping and meddling in American affairs escalated. Outrage and hatred were chronicled in the song "When the *Lusitania* Went Down." The *Lusitania*, a U.S. passenger liner, had been sunk by a German submarine on May 1, 1915. Still, the songwriters urged peace with songs like "The Hero of the European War," which praised Wilson for keeping America out of the war, and "Don't Forget That He's Your President," a plea to stand by the president's neutrality position.

By 1917, German U-boats had sunk eight American ships. There was no avoiding the fact that this was an act of war. With tears in his eyes, President Wilson signed a declaration of war on April 6, saying to one of his aides, "My message today was a message of death for our young men."

Immediately, popular music reflected and capitalized on the new national mood. Tin Pan Alley had developed into an efficient machine. If the country demanded a particular type of song, the Alley could produce it. And the demand for war songs was phenomenal. There were songs of sentiment and nostalgia, harking back to the traditions of earlier decades. The cover of "Till We Meet Again" depicts a soldier bidding a touching farewell to his lady love before going off to war. "Just a Baby's Prayer at Twilight (For Her Daddy Over There)" shows an angelic child kneeling in prayer with her doll at her side. The cover was designed by Albert Barbelle, whose work appeared frequently during the war years and beyond. "Roses of Picardy," a British import, was an extremely popular ballad that expressed sentiments of wartime parting. Other frequently sung sentimental ballads were "The Little Grey Mother Who Waits All Alone," "When You Come Back," and "So Long, Mother."

The *Lusitania* was not forgotten, either. The enemy figured in numerous songs. "We're Going to Knock the 'Hel' Out of Wilhelm—and It Won't Take Us Long," "When the Kaiser Does the Goose-Step to a Good Old American Rag," and "If He Can Fight Like He Can Love, Good Night, Germany!" are examples of songs created both to ridicule and to inspire hate. Many of the song covers carried cartoonlike depictions of the Kaiser, portraying him as a soldier-buffoon. The lyrics left nothing to the imagination.

America had to laugh too. Soldiers laughed as they slogged through mud and cold, humming "How Ya Gonna Keep 'Em Down on the Farm (After They've Seen Paree?)"; "Would You Rather Be a Colonel with an Eagle on Your Shoulder, or a Private With a Chicken on Your Knee?"; "I'd Like to See the Kaiser with a Lily in His Hand"; and "Oh! What a Time for the Girlies When the Boys Come Marching Home."

Songs about allied countries and their citizens abounded—"Lorraine My Beautiful Alsace Lorraine," "Oh Frenchy!" and "When Yankee Doodle Learns to Parlez Vous Francais." These tunes emphasized the friendship between the lands, sparking the comradeship so necessary in times of conflict. The cover of "Goodbye, Broadway, Hello, France" shows soldiers of the two countries shaking hands across the ocean.

Some of the war's most memorable songs began as part of fund-raising efforts. Perhaps the most enduring and endearing song of Word War I was "Over There." George M. Cohan read the headlines of America's entry into the war and quickly penned the tune. It was introduced in the fall of 1917 at a Red Cross benefit at the Hippodrome in New York City and was an instant success. "Over There" sold more than two million copies of sheet music and over one million recordings. It was even recorded by the great opera singer Enrico Caruso. Among those who illustrated covers for different issues of the song were Barbelle and Norman Rockwell. Rockwell's cover is desirable both for its striking depiction of young soldiers absorbed in song and for its rarity.

Cohan, long known as an ardent patriot, donated all of his royalties from the song to war charities. Its impact on the country did not go unnoticed in high places, for it eventually earned him a congressional medal by a special act of Congress.

Songwriter Irving Berlin, a member of the army, was also involved in fund-raising efforts. His commanding officer asked him to create and produce an all-soldier show to raise money for a service center. The result, *Yip, Yip, Yaphank*, created a sensation at New York's Century Theatre in 1918. Berlin headed a cast that performed such entertaining numbers as

"Oh, How I Hate to Get Up in the Morning." The project's initial goal of $35,000 was far exceeded: it earned $38,000 in New York alone, and a brief tour brought the proceeds up to $150,000.

The flurry of war activity included concerted conservation efforts. Not only fuel and food, but paper, too, needed to be saved, which had a direct impact on sheet music. The traditional large format gave way to the standard size still in present use. Smaller and miniature sizes were also produced, the latter a lucky find for the collector.

To support the war effort, the Treasury Department issued War Savings Stamps with the slogan "Lick the stamps and lick the Kaiser." Liberty Loan bond issues were highly successful. The government's fund-raising and recruiting drives were accompanied by more patriotic songs. "Liberty Bell, It's Time to Ring Again" went one, while "Buy a Liberty Bond for the Baby" went another. Others were "It's Your Country and My Country"; "America, Here's My Boy," by Andrew B. Sterling and Arthur Lange; "If I Had a Son for Each Star in Old Glory," said to be an ideal recruiting song for Uncle Sam; "I'll Do the Same As My Daddy"; "They Didn't Go Back on Uncle Sam"; and "Lafayette—We Hear You Calling," a pledge of support for France.

The behind-the-scenes heroics of the Red Cross nursing staff were not overlooked in song. "I Don't Want to Get Well (I'm in Love with a Beautiful Nurse)" and "My Red Cross Girlie (The Wound Is Somewhere in My Heart)" record their place in the hearts of the country.

Black Americans also fought in the war, a fact often ignored by history books, though not necessarily by music publishers. Songs such as "When the Good Lord Makes a Record of a Hero's Deed He Draws No Color Line," with music by Harry De Costa, composer of "The Little Grey Mother Who Waits All Alone," and "Goodbye My Chocolate Soldier Boy" reflect black Americans' participation in the war.

Some of the songs black soldiers sang came from word of mouth and were passed from soldier to soldier. Others came from printed sheet music and were subsequently changed by use and the effects of geographic and ethnic origin. A song sung in France during the winter of 1917–1918 and recorded by John Jacob Niles was called "Going Home Song" and went, in part: "I want to go home—I want to go home—/ The treatment is awful—the food is a joke—/ If you want to pass out, just come here and you'll croak. . . . / It's always a raining—the mud is knee-deep—/ The lice are so active, I never can sleep—/ So send me over the sea/ Where the top sergeants can't get at

A 1915 doughboy.

me—/ Oh, my, I'm too young to die—/ I want to go home."

One of the most popular songs of the war, "Mademoiselle from Armentiers," was sung by black units with "Inky Dinky, parlez-vous" replacing "Hinkey-Dinkey" and such new verses as "Mademoiselle from Armentiers, parlez-vous,/ Mademoiselle from Armentiers, parlez-vous,/ I wouldn't give my high brown belle/ For every mademoiselle dis side o' hell—/ Inky Dinky, parlez-vous."

The sprightly patriotism and sentimental songs of home gradually began to give way to weary feelings as the fighting neared its end. The world was tired of war, and so was the country. Perhaps this is why the song "The World Is Waiting for the Sunrise" became so popular. It offered hope to those looking for an end to their miseries.

For four years and a hundred days the world was caught in the terrible iron grip of the Great War. Twenty million wounded and countless European cities in ruins bore testament to the horrors of modern warfare. American doughboys came back more sophisticated, more cynical. The war rocked the country's prewar foundations; in many ways—political, industrial, religious, social—America was turned upside down. Certainly it had lost its innocence. Much of a whole generation was dead or maimed, just as President Wilson had predicted.

The songs to come of the twenties and thirties reflected the loss of youth and naiveté. The ragtime of former days turned into jazz—a distortion of conventional musical methods and forms. The country's social mores strayed from convention as well. The war had been a bridge between the lighter, nostalgic turn of the century to a more complex world of intricate politics, lifestyles, and corruption. The Roaring Twenties was on its way.

Lyrics and cover feature the Kaiser as a viperous monster, his soldiers as swine, and his flag as a "dirty rag." Song and cover were designed to whip up a patriotic frenzy in the most doubting heart (1918).

A patriotic war support song with a superb cover by DeTakacs.

Above: The anthem of every tired doughboy (1918).

Above left: One of the many World War I "mother" songs. This cover featured the singer Al Jolson.

A popular World War I hit with a rousing chorus.

"Take Your Girlie to the Movies"

SONGS OF THE SILENT SCREEN

RARELY HAS A TIME IN ENTERTAINMENT HISTORY had such far-reaching impact as the silent movie era. It marked the birth of a major American leisure pastime, not to mention a lucrative business industry.

The silent movies also spawned a colorful variety of unique song sheets. Movie theme songs, tunes about the screen stars, ordinary songs with glamorous promotional star portraits—all helped to popularize the new industry and, ultimately, to provide a fascinating array for the collector.

The movies were born in 1892 in New Jersey when Thomas A. Edison found a way to project moving pictures onto a screen large enough to be viewed by more than one or two people. Edison opened the Thomas Edison New Kinegraphic Theater in West Orange, New Jersey, the first "movie studio."

Moving pictures were first seen in places called penny arcades or peep shows. These were usually storerooms decorated with posters and stills. To see

One of the many star depictions on sheet-music covers from the days of the silent screen (1919).

"moving pictures," one dropped a penny in a slot, looked into an aperture, and ground a crank. At the same time, one could listen to a phonographic accompaniment. The whole show lasted about a minute.

Then, with the invention of a crude projector, large audiences in music halls and vaudeville houses began enjoying one- or two-minute portrayals of dancers, acrobats, natural wonders, parades, and the like.

In 1895, the song slide was conceived. Actors and actresses were photographed in dramatic or tearjerking scenes. These pictures were placed on slides and projected on a screen while a song was sung. They were immediately successful. There were mainly two types of illustrated songs, the ballad and the march, and both had to tell a story so they could be illustrated. The songs and slides gave variety to the "movie" program and they cost the theater owner only the slide rental. Often, the house pianist did the singing as part of his regular job. Some of the better houses, however, had regular stage singers. On these occasions, song pluggers were always welcome to croon or lead audiences in singing such popular hits as "Dreaming of You" and "Without a Wedding Ring."

Some of the more popular illustrated songs of the period were "The Little Lost Child," "A Bird in a Gilded Cage," "Hello Central, Give Me Heaven," "On the Banks of the Wabash," "Mother Was a Lady," "Break the News to Mother," "When You Know You're Not Forgotten, By the Girl You Can't Forget," and "Trust Him Not the Gypsy Fortune Teller Said." The sheet-music covers for these songs were produced in large size and illustrated by artists Edward H. Pfeiffer and Albert Barbelle, among others, although photographs of popular singers or entertainers were sometimes featured.

Before 1900, screen-projected movies were practically a monopoly of vaudeville theaters, but they began losing favor as their newness wore off. Then, in 1903, came *The Great Train Robbery*, written, produced, and photographed by Edwin S. Porter and shot in Dover, New Jersey. It actually told a story, and included horseback chases, a robbery, and exciting fight scenes. Audiences were astounded and breathless with anticipation, and the movies were established as a major source of entertainment. Nickelodeon theaters usually showed four to six one-reel movies and three songs with slides. They blossomed all over the country, and by 1907 there were some four hundred in operation.

Nickelodeons offered a wonderful place for song pluggers from publishing houses to introduce new songs from Tin Pan Alley. The pianist was encouraged to work the new song into the scores of movies and to play it over and over, thereby bulldozing it into the consciousnesses of moviegoers.

Soon the nickelodeon theaters became a home away from home for the whole family. Singers led the audience in song while scenes illustrating the lyrics were thrown on the screen. And then came the movies themselves. Magic had entered the lives of ordinary people.

As these movies began to develop into a popular novelty, several new manufacturing firms sensed impending opportunities. Not only did they begin to build and refine general film techniques, they also monopolized equipment rentals and film sales. These firms, namely Edison, Biograph, and Vitagraph, began a booming business with vaudeville houses of the day.

Bitter competition between the three major companies flourished, and newly developing independent firms added to the confusion. The competition had several interesting outcomes. One was the move from New York and its environs to Hollywood, California, and the latter's development as the center of film production. The creation of the star system followed shortly.

In 1907, most films were still produced like plays: static, with the players at a fixed distance from the camera. The director D. W. Griffith departed from this practice by moving his camera nearer and nearer to the actors. Some of Griffith's stars whom the public got its first close look at were Mary Pickford, Mabel Normand, and Mae Marsh. All were eventually featured on sheet-music covers, most notably Mabel Normand, whose face graced the cover of the sheet featuring the first theme song written especially for a movie. That was "Mickey," for Mack Sennett's photoplay of the same name, produced in 1918.

Prior to 1910, the growing number of movie fans could identify their favorite stars only through studio name or roles portrayed—"The Biograph Girl" or "The Man with the Sad Eyes," for example. Most studios feared that if the performers gained too much personal notoriety, they would demand higher salaries.

Soon, however, there was a long list of performers who proved major box-office attractions—Lillian Gish, John Bunny, Blanche Sweet, and Douglas Fairbanks, to name a few. Screen stars such as these were promoted through posters, postcards, photographs, fan magazines, and sheet music. The last did much to build both the film and music industries.

Music had always been a part of silent films; everything from pit orchestras to organs or pianos played anything from formal scores for *Birth of a Nation* to informally improvised background themes setting the mood of a scene. The popular song sheets that appeared in conjunction with the silents and their stars did more than act as a background. They served in the forefront to publicize and popularize an industry that the public found infinitely fascinating.

Stars appeared in striking photographs on sheet-music covers, although there did not apparently have to be a connection between the song and the star. Evidently the advertising for star, song, and film company was connection enough. The 1914 rendition of "In the Evening by the Moonlight in Dear Old Tennessee" featured King Baggot, star of such early flicks as *Ivanhoe*, *The Scarlet Letter*, and *Dr. Jekyll and Mr. Hyde*. The same year Francis X. Bushman, "pin-up boy of the silents," appeared on "One Wonderful Night: A Hesitation Waltz." The 1919 copy of "I'm

"America's Sweetheart" helped the sales of sheet music (1914).

Right: Beautiful screen star Marion Davies on the cover of a 1919 sheet.

Left: An exotic locale and passionate romance are enticingly portrayed on this cover.

This song, which mentions the likes of Jessie Lasky, Theda Bara, Charlie Chaplin, and Mary Pickford, directly reflects the creation of Hollywood and the developing star system.

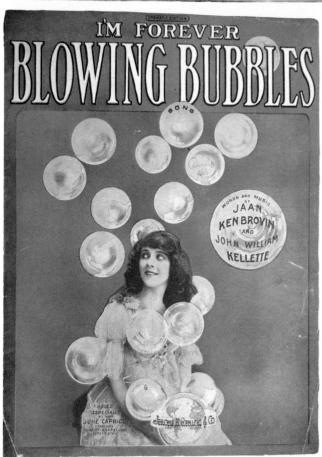

"Bubbling" June Caprice adorns the cover of a 1919 hit.

In this song to silent star Theda Bara, a man escapes from her "vamp" wiles by declaring he will not be lured by her "magic powers" (1916).

Broken Blossoms

Lyric by
BALLARD MACDONALD

Music by
A. ROBERT KING

THIS NUMBER ON ALL
PHONOGRAPH RECORDS
AND MUSIC ROLLS

POSED BY
MISS MARION DAVIES

Published by Shapiro, Bornstein & Co. MUSIC PUBLISHERS
Cor. 47th St. & Broadway
New York

A cover of 1915 featured the Little Tramp.

Forever Blowing Bubbles" charmingly portrayed June Caprice, star of *Every Girl's Dream* and *A Damsel in Distress*; Mrs. Jane Jennings, a Vitagraph star, was pictured on the cover of "That Wonderful Mother of Mine."

Film companies naturally did not miss an opportu-nity to get some billing on the sheet music. In addition to Edison, Biograph, and Vitagraph, companies such as Famous Players Film Company, Mack Sennett, IMP, Majestic, Reliance, and Selig found their way onto the covers of song sheets.

As the popularity of screen stars took greater hold,

songs were introduced about the stars themselves or the characters they portrayed. Mary Pickford was introduced by Biograph director Griffith and subsequently stolen by IMP. One of the most enduring screen personalities who always seemed to star as a sweet, innocent girl, Pickford was the featured subject of the 1914 song "Mary Pickford: The Darling of Them All."

Another immortal screen star was remembered in "That Charlie Chaplin Walk" of 1915. Chaplin also composed songs himself. "The Peace Patrol" and "Oh That Cello" of 1916 are examples. "Sing a Song," linked with his 1925 silent *The Gold Rush,* was co-written with Abe Lyman and Gus Arnheim and, of course, pictured Charlie on the cover.

The Perils of Pauline was a famous 1914 serial picture in which the heroine performed death-defying stunts to unravel mysteries and save her life. In true cliff-hanger tradition, star Pearl White managed to keep the audience on the edge of their seats. "Poor Pauline" and "Pauline Waltz" commemorated the intrepid Pauline.

Theme-song covers advertised the movie with which they were associated by showing the stars on the cover. There were some exceptions, however. For example, "The Birth of a Nation" (1915) was large-sized and had a drawing of an unidentified man and woman on the cover.

Silent stars featured on movie-theme covers included Pola Negri in *Bella Donna,* her first American picture; Norma Talmadge in *Ashes of Vengeance;* Vilma Banky in *The Awakening* (the song was "Marie"); and Corinne Griffith in *Black Oxen* (the song was "When Romance Wakes").

Other famous silent film stars pictured on song-sheet covers were Theda Bara, John Barrymore, Richard Barthelmess, Clara Bow, William Boyd, Louise Brooks, Francis X. Bushman, Dolores Costello, William and Dustin Farnum, Greta Garbo, John Gilbert, Dorothy and Lillian Gish, William S. Hart, Rod La Rocque, Harold Lloyd, Colleen Moore, Mae Murray, Ramon Novarro, Wallace Reid, Norma Shearer, Gloria Swanson, Blanche Sweet, Constance Talmadge, Ben Turpin, Rudolph Valentino, and Clara Kimball Young.

Prior to World War I, both music and films possessed a certain air of innocence. Simple stories of good versus evil, carefree songs of sentimental feelings, portrayals of classic tales, or tunes about everyday hardships predominated.

As time went by, especially after the war, the country's experience expanded along with its interests. More sophisticated humor, exoticism, passion, intrigue, and even sexy chorus lines began augmenting the previous realm of movie lore. Film music naturally reflected the trend. As Rudolph Valentino's sheik and Theda Bara's vamp along with newly discovered exotic locales gained nationwide attention, echoes were found both in the content and on the covers of such songs as "Dardanella" and "The Sheik of Araby."

Once the Roaring Twenties emerged, an emphasis on more sophisticated and daring modes of living led to songs like "The Flapper Wife." Mack Sennett, famous for his slapstick Keystone comedies, introduced flashy lines of bathing beauties. This prompted Ray Perkins's 1919 tune "Help! Help! Mr. Sennett. I'm Drowning in a Sea of Love."

Lifestyles of stars, directors, and movie magnates alike loomed larger than ever. Lavish parties, glamorous outings, glittering romances and rivalries, and popular star antics were hungrily followed by the public. This was reflected in the 1920 song "At the Moving Picture Ball," which managed to mention Theda Bara, Jessie Lasky, Douglas Fairbanks, and Mary Pickford, among others, in its sly and bouncy lyrics.

Theme songs rapidly gained in popularity. What better way to promote film, star, and song all in one vehicle? The first film with a fully synchronized musical score was Warner's *Don Juan,* starring John Barrymore, in 1926. The year before, composer William Axt had written music for the silent films *The Big Parade* and *Ben Hur,* starring Ramon Novarro and Francis X. Bushman. All had sheet music issued in conjunction with their release. *School Days, Smilin' Through,* and *Ramona,* a big hit starring Dolores Del Rio, followed the trend.

By 1926, popular songs written directly for the movies rivaled the popularity of those for the stage. In 1926 the song was "Charmaine," from the film *What Price Glory,* featuring Dolores Del Rio; in 1927 it was "Diane," from *Seventh Heaven,* with Janet Gaynor and Charles Farrell on the cover; and in 1928 it was "Jeaninne, I Dream of Lilac Time" from *Lilac Time,* starring Colleen Moore.

The movie theme song was so popular that it may have, ironically, spelled the end of the silents. Warner Brothers began experimenting with Vitaphone process in order to synchronize theme with movie. It produced a form of sound film consisting of a projector hooked to a phonograph record. Movietone was another version of this process.

On October 6, 1927, Warner presented *The Jazz Singer.* Al Jolson starred. He sang and talked, and the rest is history. The picture grossed $3 million, an unprecedented sum for that time, and the era of silent films was over.

Getting from one place to the other (1908).

Innovations, large and small, were reason enough to write a song. This one from 1905 is probably the boardwalk in Atlantic City, New Jersey.

"Why Don't You Try (The Rolling Chair)"

MISCELLANY

A WEALTH OF SHEET MUSIC WAS PUBLISHED during the late nineteenth and early twentieth centuries through the 1920s. Music publishers could push any tune if it had a colorful, topical, or innovative cover. And a variety of categories with intriguing designs, the likes of which were not to be seen again, were produced by the thousands.

Beautiful girls were depicted on countless covers.

"Peggy O' Neil," "Carmenella," "A Pretty Girl Is Like a Melody," "My Little Girl," and "Drifting" are examples, with their cover paintings of lovely women. Vivid portraits of idealized Indian maidens were also popular on songs written in tribute to them.

Songs about inventions or innovations that had become the rage abounded. Titles and covers paid homage to the automobile—"My Merry Oldsmobile,"

"He'd Have to Get Under, Get Out and Get Under, to Fix Up His Automobile," "Give Me a Spin in Your Mitchell Bill," "Henry's Made a Lady Out of Lizzy," "Home James (Don't Spare the Horses)," and "The Little Ford Ambled Right Along"—the airplane— "Come Josephine in My Flying Machine" and "Take Me Up with You Dearie"—the telephone—"The Telephone Girl" and "Hello Central, Give Me Heaven"—and the telegraph—"Atlantic Telegraph Polka." National heroes such as Charles Lindbergh, the first aviator to fly solo across the Atlantic, for whom more than one hundred songs were written, were also often depicted on sheet-music covers.

Other transportation modes, including sailing ships, and railroad, steamships, trolleys, and buses were featured on song sheets and included such gems as "The Faithful Engineer" and "Kansas Pacific RW Grand March," whose earlier lithographed covers are truly beautiful. Others included "That Railroad Rag," "The Chicago Express March and Two Step," and "Waitin' for the Train to Come In."

Bicycling took America by storm for the last third of the nineteenth century, and sheet-music covers depicting the fad proliferated. Early ones, such as "Velocipede Polka" (1869) and "Velocipedia" (1868), both featured vignettes of riders on their lithographed covers. By 1890, the bicycle looked much as it does today, and was pictured with its rider on covers such as "The Bicycle Girl" (1890), "The Cycle King" (1896), and "Get Your Lamps Lit" (1895), which showed a lantern that could be attached to the front of the bike.

Baseball, America's national sport and obsession, descended from the English game rounders as well as from cricket, was played in England in the 1830s and organized in the United States in 1845. The New York Knickerbockers were the first official baseball club in America, and they played their first game in 1846 in Hoboken, New Jersey. According to Lester Levy, the 1860 lithograph "Live Oak Polka" is the first colored lithograph for sheet music showing a

Western writer Bret Harte's adventure stories were the inspiration for this 1870 cover. Chinese, who had been brought into the West to work on the railroads, were often the subject of derision and discrimination for their dress and customs. *Collection of Dr. Danny O. Crew*

Any leisure pastime might find its way into song.

This comic cover heralded the popularity—and unreliability—of the newfangled automobile.

This cover features a famous stage comedian and female impersonator from 1868.

baseball scene. The Rochester Live Oaks were the depicted team.

Hundreds of examples have been produced since then. Earlier ones were dedicated to local teams. "The Red Stockings" (1869) is an example, with its striking cover engravings of the undefeated players circled around pitcher Asa Brainard. Since 1876, almost every great or beloved team has been pictured on song sheets, and the players who caught the public's fancy have had their turns as well. Babe Ruth's picture has appeared on ten covers, and Ty Cobb, Honus Wagner, Lou Gehrig, Joe DiMaggio, and Hank Aaron, among many others, have all been pictured. Songs about baseball on sheet-music covers include "Take Me Out to the Ball Game" (1908), "The Grand Old Game of Baseball" (1912), "That Baseball Rag" (1913), "Joltin' Joe DiMaggio" (1941), "I Want to Go to the Ball Game" (1913), and "Why Do They All Pick on Brooklyn" (1945).

College music, and particularly football, was the inspiration for many song sheets. While the first game of football was played in 1840, it wasn't until 1894 that "The Yale March" was written. "The Winning Touchdown," a Harvard song, followed in 1895, and between 1901 and 1911 the college football song blossomed. Yale's "Boola," Dartmouth's "As the Backs Go Tearing By," Brown's "Victory March," "Cheer for Old Amherst," and "The Georgia Tech March" are a few. Cornell's "Far Above Cayuga's Waters," Maine's "Stein Song," and Georgia's "Ramblin' Wreck" are others. Later songs commemorating college life included "Betty Coed" and "All American Girl."

The Spanish-American War was the catalyst for another outburst of topical songs. The theme of the reunion of the North and South to fight a common enemy was echoed in such songs as "We'll All Be with You Uncle Sam" and "The Blue and the Gray at Santiago (March)." Other songs about the conflict included "My Father Was a Sailor on the *Maine*" (which ship exploded and sank in Havana Harbor), "Our Flag Waves Not Spain's," and "Liberty and Free Cuba."

Other categories abound and include songs about fairs, catastrophes—"Death Song of the Titanic," "Heroes of the Titanic," "Homeless Tonight," and "Bring Back Our Darling" (about a kidnapping case) —children, flowers, and people in the news. Despite their often tragic themes, these songs chronicle a gentler time in our history, and their carefully created covers pay tribute to a bygone era.

Any sport, from baseball to bicycling to golf, might show up on a sheet-music cover.

War and patriotism were always popular themes for songs and covers. This song was written by
Monroe H. Rosenfeld, the man who named Tin Pan Alley.

"BROADWAY MELODY"

"Give My Regards to Broadway"

The tradition of the American musical stage is a rich one. It echoes with many names, including those of great composers, songs, and stars. Musical theater as we know it today is a result of the blending of many different American musical performance styles. The three that played the major developmental role were extravaganzas, revues, and operettas. These types, honed in cities and hamlets across the country, ultimately combined to create a new art form.

American theater productions had begun to appear as early as the middle of the eighteenth century. *Flora, or a Hob in the Well,* a ballad opera, was first performed in Charleston in 1735. In the early 1800s, parodies and caricatures called burlesques were very successful. *Hamlet* in 1828 and *La Mosquita* in 1838 are examples.

Extravaganzas, spectacles containing music, impressive scenery, and innovative stage effects, originally from France and Britain, were performed in

America as early as 1824. By midcentury, the combination of exciting scene changes and stunts and music, including popular tunes of the day interpolated with "classics," had taken the fancy of the American public.

It is generally conceded that the extravaganza *The Black Crook,* which opened on September 12, 1866, at Niblo's Garden in New York City, signaled the true birth of the American musical theater. For five and a half hours, the audience was subjected to stage effects, ballets, musical production numbers, and chorus girls singing suggestive songs—all aimed at supporting the farfetched plot. The play was wildly successful and ran for more than four hundred performances. It was directly responsible for

Above: An exotic cover from a Romberg operetta.

This brightly colored cover, *left,* portrays the Ziegfeld girl as Flo Ziegfeld wanted her to be seen.

Miss Billie Burke, stage performer, was the second wife of the famed Flo Ziegfeld.

One of the endearing stars of the Follies, Fanny Brice, as she appeared in 1920.

making the extravaganza one of the most popular theater forms until the end of the century.

Other successful extravaganzas included *Evangeline*—the first time the term *musical comedy* was used—and *The Brook* (1879). Both of these shows represented an innovation—the creation of a coherent original score and book for a theatrical production.

As the extravaganza developed and became popular, another forerunner of the musical theater was also flowering. Called the revue, it grew directly both from minstrelsy, with its olio and fantasia sections of individual performances and group walk arounds, and from vaudeville or variety, performed in such places as Tony Pastor's Music Hall, with its song and dance and comedy.

Adonis (1884) has been called a musical as well as a burlesque. Its satiric portrayal of Pygmalion and its star, Henry E. Dixey, attracted audiences for 603 performances. Such burlesque treatments of plays and classic stories were to become favorites. The popular comedy team of Weber and Fields, whose talents ranged from childhood song and dance to vaudeville to Broadway, even performed a burlesque of *Barbara Frietchie* known as *Barbara Fidgety*.

The highly successful *A Trip to Chinatown* by Charles Hoyt opened in 1891. Its confusing, farcical plot met with much applause in New York and on tour as did its songs, which included "The Bowery" and "After the Ball." In 1894, George W. Lederer's *Passing Show* debuted. It was enormously successful, and by 1895, revues began to be an integral part of the New York stage.

Florodora, a British import of 1900, featured pretty girls in a musical number. They would become the toast of the town. Beautiful girls were thereafter a prominent feature of many musicals and theatrical revues and drew a huge box-office following.

In this vein, the *Ziegfeld Follies* began in 1907 and featured extravagant sets, lavishly costumed beauties, comic performers, and even Florenz Ziegfeld's enticing wife Anna Held. Respected American composers, including Irving Berlin and Jerome Kern, provided lovely songs that further enhanced the atmosphere of Ziegfeld's "beautiful girl" extravaganzas. The *Passing Shows, Earl Carroll's Vanities, George White's Scandals*, and others were of a similar type—but none had quite the popularity of the *Follies*.

The revue lasted into the 1940s and provided a context within which incredibly talented composers produced songs that are still standards today. Well-known examples are "I Just Can't Make My Eyes Behave," performed by Anna Held; "Shine on Harvest Moon," written by Nora Bayes and husband Jack

Norworth and performed by Bayes; "My Man," performed by Fanny Brice; "A Pretty Girl Is Like a Melody," by Irving Berlin; and "My Blue Heaven," by Walter Donaldson.

Another kind of revue paralleled the early development of the *Passing Shows*. These were the burlesques or extravaganzas of Ed Harrigan and Tony Hart. In 1879, with their presentation of *The Mulligan Guard*, theater history was made again. This time the shows were not interpolations, but original stories with music, by David Braham. And they were American tales, broad caricatures of ethnic minorities such as the Irish or German or black. It was life in the melting pot of New York City as lived by ordinary Americans, or, as E. J. Kahn, Jr., has said, "the habitués of the slums," that Harrigan and Hart wrote about. Productions such as *The Mulligan Guard's Picnic* and *The Mulligan Guard's Chowder* produced such songs as "The Babies on Our Block" and "Paddy Duffy's Pail."

George M. Cohan owed a great debt to Harrigan and Hart. As a young man he was much influenced by their productions, but he emphasized the American aspect instead of the Irish and his characters were never less than paragons of patriotism and virtue. Beginning in 1901, Cohan expressed in his musicals American pride, belief in "manifest destiny," and supreme self-confidence. His "American" musical comedies were just the thing for a chauvinistic public. Cohan, cocky and self-confident, wrote his own plays, lyrics, and music and often starred in his productions as well. In 1904, he wrote and produced *Little Johnny Jones*, which included the songs "Give My Regards to Broadway" and "Yankee Doodle Boy." Other songs from Cohan productions included "Mary's a Grand Old Name" and "You're a Grand Old Flag." Between 1906 and the end of World War I, his name was synonymous with Broadway, as attested by his shows *Forty-Five Minutes from Broadway* and *The Man Who Owns Broadway*. His was the perfect voice for a country that was still innocent and naive.

The comedy team of Weber and Fields, who starred in and produced burlesque revues in their own music hall beginning in 1896, also eschewed vulgarity. They did, however, caricature Dutch characters with thick accents, and employed such luminaries as Lillian Russell to share the billing.

The final musical type to play a major role in the development of the American musical theater was the operetta. European operas and operas bouffes enchanted the American public in the 1880s and 1890s. The operettas of Jacques Offenbach, Franz Lehár, and Johann Strauss delighted audiences, as did those of Gilbert and Sullivan, whose hugely successful *H.M.S. Pinafore* is said to have been largely responsible for making theater "respectable" and acceptable for women and children in the late nineteenth century. This is not to say that women did not attend earlier —it was just not considered a ladylike activity, and women often attended the theater veiled against recognition. *Pinafore* encouraged American librettists and composers to pattern their work after Gilbert and Sullivan. *The Little Tycoon* by Willard Spenser and Reginald de Koven's *The Begum* were obviously patterned after *The Mikado*.

The Little Tycoon, with a run of five hundred performances in Philadelphia, proved that American operetta could be as popular as European. A golden age of American comic opera began with de Koven's *Robin Hood* and continued with America's great stage composer Victor Herbert. Composer of *Babes in Toyland*, *The Fortune Teller*, *Eileen*, *Mademoiselle Modiste*, *Naughty Marietta*, and *The Red Mill* among his fifty or so operettas, Herbert gave a positive American style to the form. Melodies were both simplified and lovely —"Kiss Me Again," "Ah, Sweet Mystery of Life," "Thine Alone"—and contained reduced musical complexities. Other operetta composers of note included Rudolf Friml—*The Firefly*, *Rose-Marie*, *The Three Musketeers*—Ludwig Englander, and Sigmund Romberg—*The New Moon*, *Blossom Time*, *The Student Prince*, *The Desert Song*. The era of operetta ended about 1930 with Romberg, but it had successfully completed the triumverate of extravaganza, revue, and operetta upon which composers were poised to build modern American musical theater.

Lighthearted romantic adventures, supported by sprightly songs and dances, dotted early musical-comedy fare. From the more lasting titles, such as *Irene* (1919), with its memorable "Alice Blue Gown," and *Sally* (1920), to the less remembered, such as *Holka-Polka* of 1925, the musical theater was growing and providing an increasingly interesting blend of offerings for the public. Of course, the variety stage was still popular. During the 1920s and 1930s, some of the greatest composers America has ever produced were working in revues, honing their skills for the masterpieces to come.

Jerome Kern first worked in Tin Pan Alley as a song plugger, accompanist in vaudeville, and rehearsal pianist. Encouraged by his employer, Harms Publishing Company, Kern began writing songs, more than a hundred of which were interpolated into Broadway musical revues. In 1914, he wrote his first full score for a musical comedy, *The Girl from Utah*. His classic

A bevy of dollies from the follies (1922).

A beautiful girl from the Ziegfeld Follies.

A song, filled with Oriental stereotypes, from a 1924 revue.

Right: This cover captures the Art Deco style and costumes of bygone days in a 1978 production.

OUR PRIVATE WORLD

Music by CY COLEMAN

Lyrics by BETTY COMDEN and ADOLPH GREEN

From the Broadway Musical "ON THE TWENTIETH CENTURY"

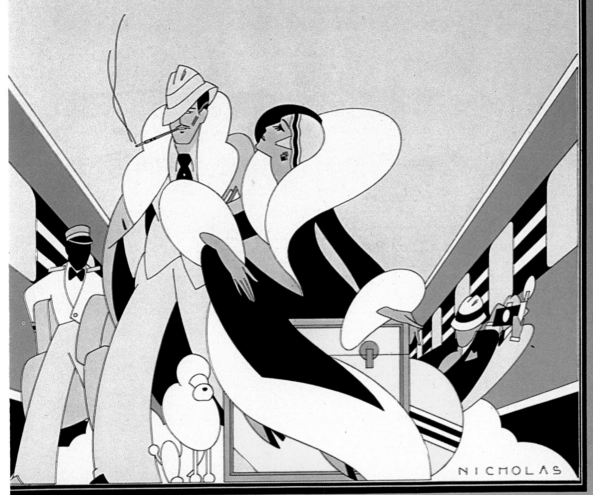

NICHOLAS

ON THE TWENTIETH CENTURY

NOTABLE MUSIC CO., INC. and
Betdolph Music Company
New York, New York

$1.50

Distributed by
big3

"They Didn't Believe Me" was written for that show. Kern, with P. G. Wodehouse and Guy Bolton, wrote *Oh, Boy* and *Oh, Lady, Lady*. As the writers for the Princess Theater Shows in New York, the trio exerted a tremendous influence. Kern's lyrical melodies shone forth in such other productions as *The Cat and the Fiddle* ("The Night Was Made for Love," "She Didn't Say 'Yes' ") and *Roberta* ("Yesterdays," "The Touch of Your Hand," "Smoke Gets in Your Eyes").

George Gershwin also wrote music for revues, beginning in 1918 when Nora Bayes performed two of his songs. In 1919, Al Jolson interpolated Gershwin's "Swanee" into his Winter Garden extravaganza *Sinbad*, and in 1920, Gershwin was asked to write the music for *George White's Scandals*. For this he produced "I'll Build a Stairway to Paradise" and "Somebody Loves Me."

Gershwin left the *Scandals* in 1924 to write for musical comedies and the concert stage. He gave us music for such twenties productions as *Oh, Kay* ("Clap Yo' Hands" and "Do, Do, Do").

Gershwin opened the thirties decade with *Strike Up the Band*. He and lyricist brother Ira wrote such memorable songs for that show as "I've Got a Crush on You," "Soon," and the title song. Later that same year, they were to hear their songs "Bidin' My Time," "Embraceable You," "I Got Rhythm," and "But Not For Me" in the production of *Girl Crazy* with Ginger Rogers and Ethel Merman. *Of Thee I Sing*—the first musical comedy to win a Pulitzer for drama—*Pardon My English, Let 'Em Eat Cake*, and *Porgy & Bess* were to follow.

Irving Berlin, already a giant in popular music, was writing for Broadway too. For revues he produced "Play a Simple Melody" (1914), "A Pretty Girl Is Like a Melody" (1919), "What'll I Do?" (1924), and "All Alone" (1924).

The all-black revue, a product of the twenties, produced *Shuffle Along*, with the hit song "I'm Just Wild About Harry," and *The Blackbirds of 1928* introduced "I Can't Give You Anything But Love, Baby." These shows represented the rejuvenation of the all-black production, which had been absent from Broadway between 1911 and 1920. All-black stage productions started with *A Trip to Coontown* (1898), which ran for three years. One of the most successful, Bert Williams and George Walker's *In Dahomey* (1903), enjoyed a long run in New York and worldwide and introduced such turn-of-the-century hits as "My Castle on the River Nile."

The great songwriting team of Richard Rodgers and Lorenz Hart first found its success in *The Garrick Gaieties* in 1925; "Mountain Greenery" followed in 1926.

Through the twenties, Rodgers and Hart were the greatest team writing for musical comedy. They produced "Thou Swell" for *A Connecticut Yankee*, "My Heart Stood Still" and "You Took Advantage of Me" for *Present Arms*, and "With a Song in My Heart" for *Spring Is Here*. By the time they again wrote for Broadway, in 1935, a new era was in progress, one they had helped create. Songs from many Rodgers and Hart hit shows are still popular. "The Most Beautiful Girl in the World" and "My Romance" (*Jumbo*), "There's a Small Hotel" and the instrumental "Slaughter on Tenth Avenue" (*On Your Toes*), and "Where or When" and "My Funny Valentine" (*Babes in Arms*) are just a few.

Cole Porter, the quintessential interpreter of the reckless abandon of the Roaring Twenties, wrote great songs for musical comedies into the 1950s. His first hit, "An Old Fashioned Garden," was written for a revue called *Hitchy-Koo of 1919*. He went on to produce *The Gay Divorcee* ("Night and Day," 1932), *Anything Goes* ("I Get a Kick Out of You," 1934), *Kiss Me Kate* ("So in Love" and "Wunderbar," 1948), *Can-Can* ("I Love Paris" and "C'est Magnifique," 1953), and *Silk Stockings* ("All of You," 1955), among many others.

Musical comedies that mirrored the trials and tribulations of the Depression years included Irving Berlin's *Face the Music*; Rodgers and Hart's *I'd Rather Be Right*; Berlin's *As Thousands Cheer*, which introduced "Easter Parade"; Kurt Weill's *Johnny Johnson*, a bitter statement against impending war; and *Pins and Needles*, a show staged by the International Ladies Garment Workers Union (ILGWU), with most of the lyrics and music by Harold Rome. A relative unknown until this production, Rome later wrote *Call Me Mister* (1946), a revue whose theme was the readjustment of soldiers to civilian life.

At its start, musical theater had consisted of a random series of musical numbers and sketches, loosely strung together to create a sometimes haphazard whole. In the twenties, however, ideas began to change. The story line became dominant, edified and glorified by pertinent song-and-dance numbers. The new art form took itself seriously, attempting to convey universal human emotions through sensitive characterization and skillful use of melody and lyrics. The musical play was born in 1927 with the production of Jerome Kern and Oscar Hammerstein II's *Show Boat*. Adapted from the novel by Edna Ferber, it was an instant hit. Critics went wild, as did audiences,

From George Gershwin and DuBose Heyward's landmark American black opera.

SUMMERTIME

THE THEATRE GUILD PRESENTS

PORGY and BESS

MUSIC BY
GEORGE GERSHWIN

LIBRETTO BY
DUBOSE HEYWARD

LYRICS BY
DUBOSE HEYWARD and IRA GERSHWIN

PRODUCTION DIRECTED BY
ROUBEN MAMOULIAN

GERSHWIN PUBLISHING CORP.
RKO BLDG. NEW YORK N.Y.
CHAPPELL & CO. INC.
SOLE SELLING AGENT
MADE IN U.S.A.

An assortment of popular programs from the 1930s and 1940s.

A 1911 song from one of the famed
Hippodrome productions.

The 1919 hit sung by the great Al Jolson.

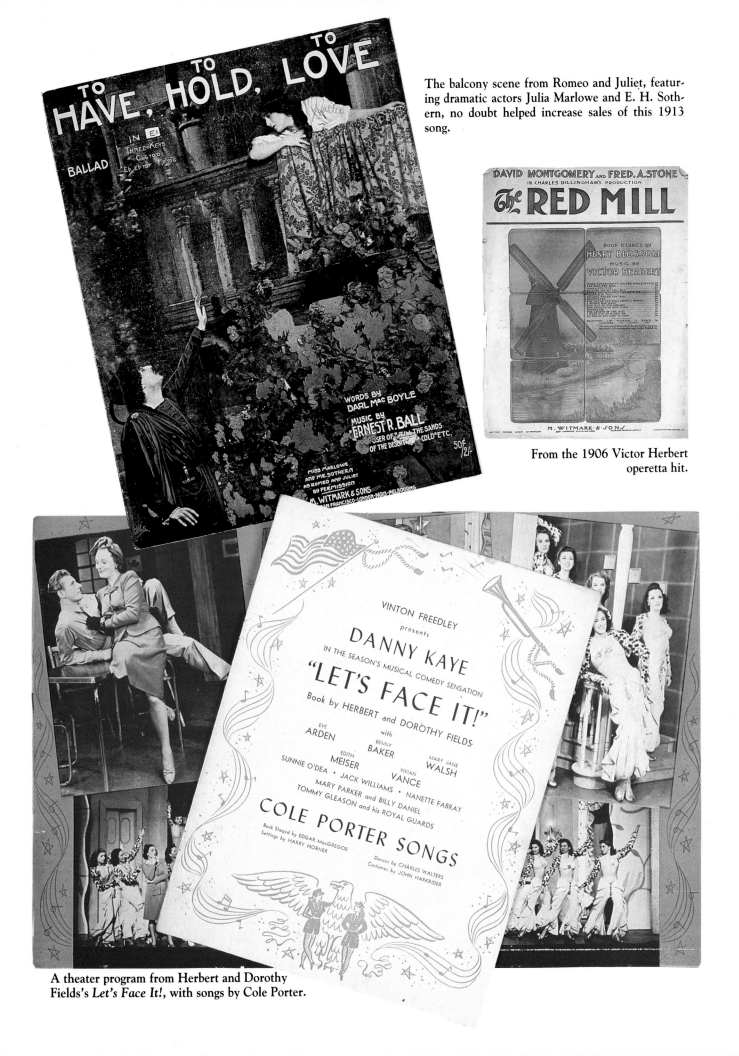

The balcony scene from Romeo and Juliet, featuring dramatic actors Julia Marlowe and E. H. Sothern, no doubt helped increase sales of this 1913 song.

From the 1906 Victor Herbert operetta hit.

A theater program from Herbert and Dorothy Fields's *Let's Face It!*, with songs by Cole Porter.

and the play's Broadway run lasted nearly two years. It was to serve as a yardstick by which future musical shows of a more "serious" nature would be judged. Among its successors were *Cabin in the Sky*, with an all-black cast; *On Your Toes*, with dances created by George Balanchine; and *Pal Joey*, by Rodgers and Hart.

A new partnership of Rodgers and Hammerstein, which lasted for seventeen years and created a magical era in musical theater, produced the musicals *Carousel*, *South Pacific*, *The King and I*, and *The Sound of Music*. *Oklahoma!*, one of the most endearing of the duo's musicals, was first produced in 1943. Fantastic choreography by Agnes de Mille brought a new artistic dimension to the vastly untapped possibilities of musical dance. The score contained such hits as "Oh, What a Beautiful Mornin'," "Out of My Dreams," and "People Will Say We're in Love."

Other mature American theater productions with fully realized emotional development were *Annie Get Your Gun* (Herbert and Dorothy Fields and Irving Berlin); *Brigadoon* and *My Fair Lady* (Alan Jay Lerner and Frederick Loewe); *Guys and Dolls* (Frank Loes-ser); *Fiddler on the Roof* (Jerry Bock and Sheldon Harnick); *West Side Story* (Leonard Bernstein and Stephen Sondheim); *Company* and *A Little Night Music* (Sondheim); *The Music Man* (Meredith Willson); *Hello, Dolly!* and *Mame* (Jerry Herman); and *Funny Girl* (Jule Styne and Bob Merrill).

In the second half of the twentieth century, American musical theater continued to evolve. Intricate scenery, experimental choreography, in-depth scripts, serious character depictions, acerbic social commentary and satire, lush musical arrangements, sophisticated lighting, elaborate special effects, high-grade direction, and advanced technology all combined to elevate the art form to a new level.

The years continue to bring their changes. Alienation has replaced archetypes—compare *Follies* to *Oklahoma!*, *A Chorus Line* to *Carousel*. Lasting song hits are no longer pouring out of Broadway. There are some exceptions, of course, such as "Send in the Clowns" from *A Little Night Music* and "Memory" from *Cats*. But many melodies today are involved in evoking the momentary emotional flow of the lyric,

A song from one of the famous Shubert brothers productions of 1906.

John Barrymore, the great dramatic actor, actually sang in this 1919 production.

"Proper" theatergoers had their *Theatre* magazine. Patrons of bawdier girlie shows had their *Standard*. This rare copy from 1901 shows Florodora girls enticingly photographed amid risqué stories and jokes.

which runs seamlessly into the dialogue in a fashion similar to that of opera. To take a modern production and fuse it with a timeless operatic form may be one of the new theatrical waves, as, for example, in *Sweeney Todd*.

And what about rock musicals—*Hair; Jesus Christ, Superstar; Godspell; Evita*? They were fresh and innovative, bridging the gap between pop music and musical theater. They had some good songs that, by virtue of enormous record sales alone, have become classics ("Don't Cry for Me, Argentina" from *Evita* and "I Don't Know How to Love Him" from *Jesus Christ, Superstar*). Time will tell whether we will be singing them in fifty years.

From *The Black Crook* to *Gypsy* to *Sunday in the Park with George*, musical theater has continued to hold its fascination for audiences. It is an ever-changing set on which lives, loves, passions, and history are played out to music, and it is, for all its faults and failures, gloriously, singularly, American.

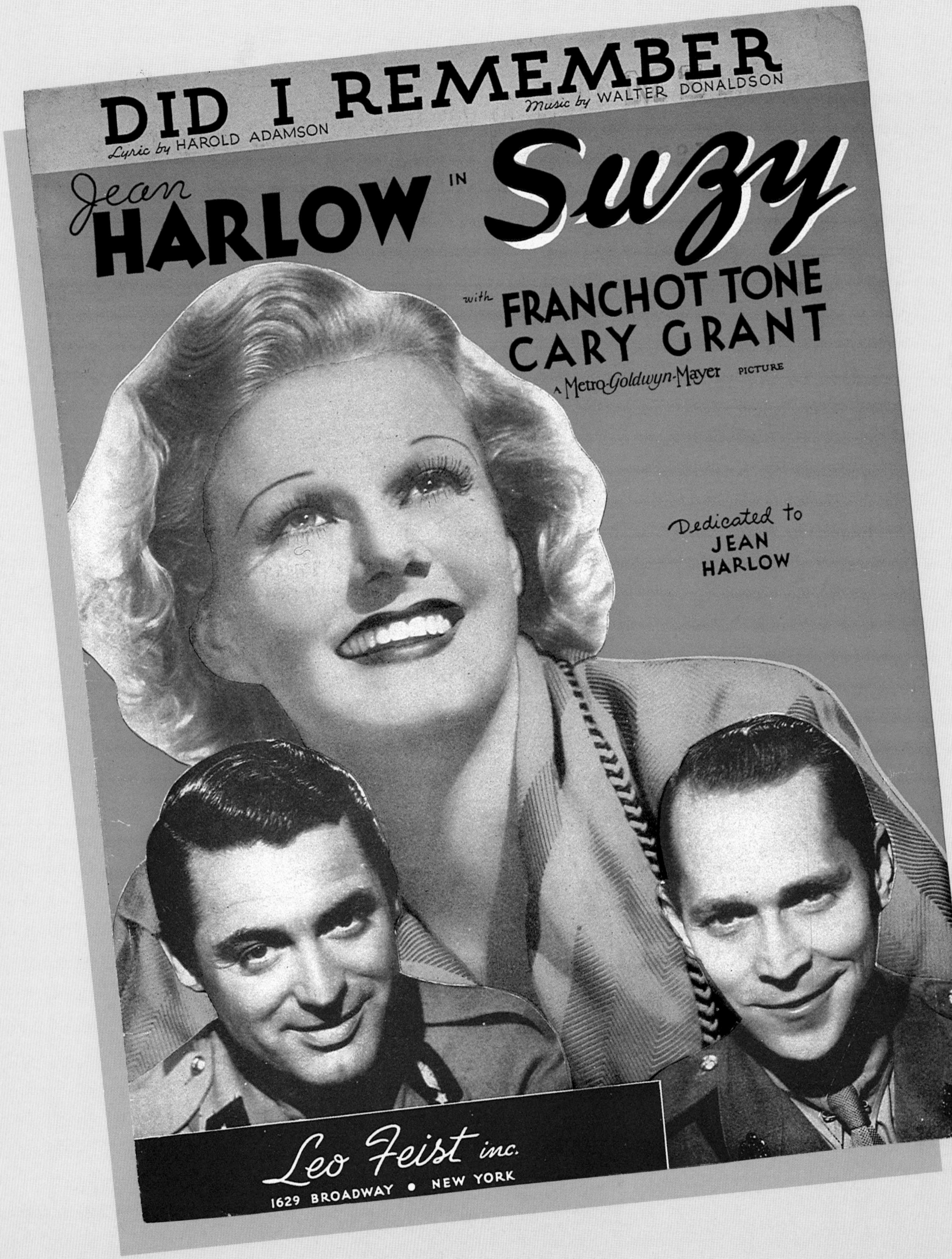
DID I REMEMBER
Lyric by HAROLD ADAMSON
Music by WALTER DONALDSON
Jean HARLOW IN Suzy
with FRANCHOT TONE
CARY GRANT
A Metro-Goldwyn-Mayer PICTURE
Dedicated to
JEAN
HARLOW
Leo Feist inc.
1629 BROADWAY • NEW YORK

"NIGHT AND DAY"

The Thirties

"Brother, Can You Spare a Dime?"

THE DEPRESSION

The year 1929 was a troubled one for America. It saw the grim St. Valentine's Day massacre in Chicago and witnessed convictions in the notorious Teapot Dome scandal.

The entertainment industry was in a state of transition, marking a turbulent era for performers. "Talkies" swept the motion-picture industry, and the shining stars of vaudeville rapidly lost their luster.

October 1929 was to be forever etched in the memories of Americans. The crash of the stock market heralded the end of the reckless abandon of the Roaring Twenties. The transformation of American life within a few short months after the crash seems astonishing, especially today with government systems as safety nets. Vast social changes occurred.

Speculators who once lived lavishly, supported by their investments, were leaping from windows. Flappers who floated from party to party were suddenly forced to wait on breadlines, and formerly successful

POTATOES ARE CHEAPER - TOMATOES ARE CHEAPER
NOW'S THE TIME TO FALL IN LOVE
by AL SHERMAN AND AL LEWIS
EDDIE CANTOR'S SMASHING HIT

businessmen, their overcoats now lined with newspapers, begged for a free meal. Women were abandoned as their husbands took to the road. Children, homeless victims of families that had disintegrated from poverty and unemployment, begged and stole, living by their wits as they wandered from town to town. Black poverty reached an all-time high and racial tensions deepened in a land where jobs were prized above all else. Factories stopped producing what people had no money to buy, and in the great, formerly rich, central American farm belt, dust decimated the land. The Great Depression had arrived.

It was a turning point in the maturing of the country and a turning point for its musical maturity as well.

Above: Eddie Cantor's hit of 1931.

Left: Famous stars were featured on sheet music throughout the thirties. Many of the songs were theme songs from otherwise straight dramas as well as musicals (1936).

Popular songs of the day reflected the nation's deep trouble—an unemployment rate of 10 million by the end of 1931 and some 2,300 bank failures.

Yet there was also a voice of confidence that managed to shine through. By November 1929, everyone was desperately singing "Happy Days Are Here Again." Recorded on Black Tuesday, October 29, 1929, its upbeat lyrics and promise of prosperity "just around the corner" gave Americans an outlet for their natural tendency to look on the bright side. Songs such as "Get Happy," "Help Yourself to Happiness," and "On the Sunny Side of the Street" also tried to inject a brighter outlook during bleak times and a hope that tomorrow would be better.

In truth, though, it would be many long years before the country recovered, and initial optimism sometimes gave way to questions about the system and about American morality. All this was reflected in the songs people sang.

"Headin' for Better Times," written in 1931 by Mencher and Tobias, was the kind of upbeat, hummable number that kept spirits up at first. Maybe you couldn't completely ignore the world falling around your ears, but you could drown out the pain of it with songs like "Dancing in the Dark," "Life Is Just a Bowl of Cherries," and "Let's Put Out the Lights and Go to Sleep," which encouraged people to ignore their troubles and not dwell on the negative side of life. Other attempts to mask hard times included "(Potatoes Are Cheaper, Tomatoes Are Cheaper) Now's the Time to Fall in Love" (Lewis, Sherman); "I Found a Million Dollar Baby" (Warren, Rose, Dixon); "Cheerful Little Earful" (Gershwin, Rose, Warren), which suggested that even if stocks go down and business slows down, a simple "I love you" will make everything fine; "I Got Rhythm" (the Gershwins), a musical tour de force which stated that money was the least important item one could, or should, need to be happy; and "The Gold Diggers' Song (We're in the Money)" (Dubin, Warren) from *42nd Street*, which had dancing girls tapping and singing about better times after finding a dime in the street.

Musical form and the scope of influence upon the popular repertoire gained new breadth during this time. The self-centered, almost adolescent quality of former days gave way to more maturely sophisticated realms of musical exploration.

The wild and exuberant jazz of the previous decade developed into the controlled, more formally arranged "swing." The arranger became a respected and recognized contributor in musical presentations. Bands figured prominently, performing renditions that displayed the performers' skills as well as the ar-ranger's talents. Many songs that they performed, especially the "theme" songs that became associated with each particular group, were indicative of the times. Bert Lown and his Hotel Biltmore orchestra became linked with "Bye Bye Blues," another attempt to shower optimism on weary listeners.

A growing attraction developed for Latin American music, perhaps because it represented an escape from the grim realities of everyday life into something more pleasantly exotic. Tunes such as "The Peanut Vendor" became favorites. The music of Cuban composer Ernesto Lecuona became popular as well. "Siboney" and "Say Si Si" were among his memorable melodies.

An increasing interest in popularizing the classics arose. The Czech composer Zdeněk Fibich's "Poeme" for violin was transformed into "My Moonlight Madonna," and "In the Valley of the Moon" was based upon a portion of a Mendelssohn violin concerto. This served as another indicator of widening musical experimentation and maturation both because of and despite hard times.

Certain songs were specifically linked with the problems of the Depression. Rodgers and Hart's "I've Got Five Dollars," with its mention of "debts beyond endurance," is an example.

The spring and summer of 1933 were dry; autumn was hot. Dust began to blow, a black cloud that darkened the sky over Chicago and New York State. It blew all autumn and winter, whirling precious topsoil out to sea, killing farm animals, and creating an ominous darkness at noon. Finally, despairingly, farmers abandoned their land. "Okies" and blacks from the impoverished South trekked to the cities. The farmers found mostly hatred in the Western cities and towns they came to in droves. And blacks found an unemployment rate of 50 percent in Northern cities and rising bigotry which percolated amid the sharpening racial competition for jobs.

Tragedy could not be ignored and, just as Americans used song to ignore their plight, they also used it to define and identify it. Cole Porter's "Love for Sale" touchingly tells the story of a bad-luck, good girl who must work the streets to get by. Casucci, Caesar, and Brammer's "Just a Gigolo" touches on the same theme from the man's point of view. "A Cottage for Sale" by Robison and Conley, popularized by torch singer Ruth Etting, despairs over lost dreams; "Underneath the Arches," by Connelly, Flanaga, and McCarthy, tells of the homeless sleeping under a bridge dreaming of better times; and ASCAP's award-winning song of 1934, Duke Ellington's "Solitude," evokes feelings of loss and melancholy.

There were, of course, specifically protest songs,

songs which grew out of American folk tradition and, by virtue of their timeless appeal, crossed over for a while into the popular genre. Mountain songs, labor anthems, and Woody Guthrie's Dust Bowl Ballads could be counted among them. But mostly, Americans were listening to the radio and dancing in ballrooms to an incredible outpouring of great popular music, and Tin Pan Alley had never been busier.

The quintessential Depression song, one that combined elements of folk and protest music yet managed to appeal as well to the masses, was the great "Brother, Can You Spare a Dime?" by E. Y. Harburg and Jay Gorney. Written in 1932 and popularized by Bing Crosby, its heartbreaking sense of history and appeal to fair play seemed to summarize what many were feeling. A similar appeal was made in the song "Remember My Forgotten Man," a blues-influenced piece wherein a woman laments that after having served in wartime, her man, along with her, is now forgotten.

And as moving in its own way, the Depression from one woman's point of view was evoked in "Ten Cents a Dance" (Rodgers and Hart), wherein a young woman makes a living selling dances in a tawdry ballroom to any rough sailor or tough stevedore while trying to believe that Mr. Right may still come along.

As always, songwriters could not resist poking fun at the whole situation. "Are You Makin' Any Money?" suggested that this was the only important question to be asked before marriage. "W.P.A." was a cynical commentary on one of the New Deal's many efforts to get America back on its feet.

Rodgers and Hart's "Hallelujah, I'm a Bum" celebrated the hobo's life with tongue in cheek as it chorused, "Why work away for wealth/ When you can

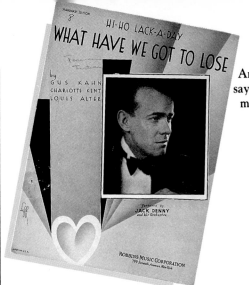

An eager suitor says why not get married despite hard times.

travel for your health/ The road is your escape/ The earth your little dinner plate."

Things did get better. As the country got back on its feet, people began to feel that they were not merely whistling in the dark, but had real reason for optimism. Songs like "Who's Afraid of the Big Bad Wolf?" by Ronell and Churchill had been a metaphor for attempts to hide the fear people felt at a world turned upside down. Later, confidence reigned in songs like "When My Ship Comes In" (Donaldson, Kahn), "With Plenty of Money and You" (Warren, Dubin), and especially "There's a New Day Comin' " (Ager, Young), which exulted in a newfound confidence that everyone would soon have a job.

The decade of the 1930s was to end with a symbolic and prophetic hit. Irving Berlin's "God Bless America" was first sung on the air by Kate Smith in 1938. It emphasized the strong spirit that had kept the country intact through the most trying of times. It also foreshadowed a patriotic resurgence that was to be necessary as America moved closer to the fearful prospect of another world war.

"I Found a Million Dollar Baby"

MOVIES

IT SEEMS ONLY NATURAL THAT A FLOWERING OF movie music would occur during the 1930s. Once sound revolutionized film making in 1927, movie studios scrambled to develop this exciting new art form. And film audiences, grim from the deprivations of the Depression, were ripe for the escapism the studios raced to give them. Individual lives may have been made tragic by starvation, unemployment, and displace-

ment, but up there on the magic screen, as darkness draped slowly around them, the movie audience could see glitter and glitz, spangled dancing shoes and beautiful gowns, songs about love and happy endings. For a few hours they could forget their cares, and when they left and were forced to face reality once again, they could still hum the songs.

The first movie musical of note was *The Broadway*

The all-American college look was a popular attraction for the moviegoing public (1934).

Below left: Child stars such as Shirley Temple became a unique phenomenon during the thirties (1936).

Below: Clark Gable and Jeanette MacDonald starred in this drama set against the backdrop of the great San Francisco earthquake (1936).

Joan Crawford was featured on this cover at the beginning of her film career (1929).

A whimsical cover portrays the stars of a 1929 musical-comedy film.

A souvenir program from the 1939 blockbuster hit. The music for the movie was written by Max Steiner.

Melody (1929), with its backstage story and catchy songs, such as the title song and "You Were Meant for Me." The great directors King Vidor, Rouben Mamoulian, and Ernst Lubitsch pushed the movie musical forward in the late twenties and early thirties by their experimentation with song. However, the medium declined in momentum in the early thirties. It took the release of 42nd Street in 1933 to bring it back to life and make the fortunes of Hollywood.

This was the first of scores of musicals with flimsy plots and characters but spectacular dance numbers and memorable tunes. Along with 42nd Street, 1933 saw Gold Diggers of 1933 and Footlight Parade, all containing glittering dance routines by Busby Berkeley. Footlight Parade's "By a Waterfall" was the first aquacade spectacular and one of the most memorable routines of these early films. Berkeley also choreographed Dames and Flirtation Walk in 1934. These films made his reputation as a uniquely imaginative creator. By using flexible, movable camera angles combined with music, he showed that a motion picture could actually be superior to a stage production and that a musical film did not have to look artificial and staged. Choruses of girl dancers performed in precise visual patterns—stars, wheels, and other shapes. Then cameras would move about, filming from above, beneath, through mirrors—all capturing the eye and the attention of the appreciative moviegoer. Spectacles like these also led to the later Esther Williams water and Sonja Henie ice feature numbers.

These musicals gave birth to the film couple, duos who were in demand again and again on the screen. Ruby Keeler and Dick Powell launched their couple career with 42nd Street and went on to Footlight Parade and other hits.

The watershed year 1933 became doubly so because it was the year Fred Astaire and Ginger Rogers danced their way into the hearts of the moviegoing public. The pictures they made together may not always have been memorable, but when Astaire and Rogers began to dance—that was when the true meaning of movie magic became evident. From 1933 to 1939, RKO teamed the two in a series of musicals, and the genre reached its apex. And the songs! Written by, among others, Cole Porter, Jerome Kern, and Otto Harbach, Irving Berlin, and the Gershwins, some of them originally for the stage, they delighted movie audiences throughout the thirties and remain classic standards today. "Night and Day," "Smoke Gets in Your Eyes," "Lovely to Look At," "Cheek to Cheek," "Let's Face the Music and Dance," "The Way You Look Tonight," "A Fine Romance," "They All Laughed," "Let's Call the Whole Thing Off," and "They Can't

Take That Away From Me" are just a few of the gems from these marvelous movies whose supremacy, certainly in the dance musical category, has never been surpassed.

Because the movie musical was so vibrant and innovative during the thirties, many of the nation's best popular songwriters, who had previously written for the stage, channeled their energies into writing for films. Mammy and Puttin' on the Ritz had songs by Irving Berlin. Others by Berlin included "Now It Can Be Told" from Alexander's Ragtime Band, and "I Used to Be Colorblind" from the 1938 Carefree. Gershwin film songs included "A Foggy Day" from A Damsel in Distress (1937), "Nice Work If You Can Get It," and "Things Are Looking Up." Richard Rodgers and Lorenz Hart's contribution to film music included "Lover," "Isn't It Romantic" and "Mimi" from the movie Love Me Tonight. "Blue Moon" was first called "Prayer" and written for Jean Harlow to sing in a film called Hollywood Revue of 1933, which was never produced. It was finally sung in the movie Manhattan Melodrama in 1934. "You Are Too Beautiful" was performed in the film Hallelujah, I'm a Bum in 1933, and "That's Love" came from the 1934 Nana.

The Cole Porter songs "Easy to Love" and "I've Got You Under My Skin" both came from the movie Born to Dance. Harold Arlen contributed "This Is Only the Beginning" and "Let's Fall in Love" to the 1933 Love Is Love, Anywhere. One of the most famous movie songs, "Over the Rainbow" from The Wizard of Oz (1939), was, if not Arlen's best, at least his most enduring song and became Judy Garland's signature song.

Other movie songs written by well-known pop music tunesmiths included "It's Been So Long" from The Great Ziegfeld (1935), "You're Getting to Be a Habit with Me" (42nd Street), "Lullaby of Broadway" (Gold Diggers of Broadway), "Summer Night" (Sing Me a Love Song), and "Jeepers Creepers" (Going Places).

Jimmy McHugh produced "I Feel a Song Comin' On" (1935) and "You're a Sweetheart" (1937). Also in 1937 came "Too Marvelous for Words" from the movie Ready, Willing, and Able, and in 1931 "I Cover the Waterfront" was written by John Green. Jimmy Van Heusen produced "All This and Heaven Too" in 1939.

More great songs from 1930s movies were "When Your Lover Has Gone" (1931), "(I Don't Stand) A Ghost of a Chance (With You)" (1932), "My Old Flame" (1934), and "You Leave Me Breathless" (1938).

The operetta translated into film with great suc-

In 1935, you could see Joan Crawford and George Raft, and at intermission you could add to your glassware collection. *Culver Pictures*

cess, popularizing the music of Romberg, Herbert, and Friml, among others. Singers Jeanette Mac-Donald and Nelson Eddy, another film couple, starred in countless productions such as *Naughty Marietta*, *Rose Marie*, and *New Moon*. The loveliness of the music and the fantasy of the plots provided sheer escape for willing moviegoers.

During the thirties, child stars were the toast of the movie studios. Audiences lapped up their innocent antics and forgot, for a while, their cares. From 1934 to 1937, Shirley Temple was the world's number-one box-office attraction, and her rendition of musical numbers left audiences wet-eyed and cheering. She began in *Stand Up and Cheer* and sang, danced, and charmed her way into America's heart throughout her childhood. She became known for such novelty songs as "Animal Crackers in My Soup" and "On the Good Ship Lollipop." Other child stars who headlined in popular films were Jackie Cooper, Deanna Durbin, Judy Garland, Dickie Moore, and Mickey Rooney.

The need for escape did not go unrecognized in Hollywood. Its launching of the double feature was met with great enthusiasm from a weary public. Two flicks for the price of one—plus a chance to win prizes between reels—proved a surefire success and an opportunity for studios to increase their profits.

Box office "blockbusters" began to be produced in the thirties. *Gone with the Wind* and *Show Boat* were enduring hits that are still loved today.

Serial movies caught on. The public would clamor for the next adventure of Charlie Chan, the Thin Man, Mr. Moto, Andy Hardy, the Marx Brothers, the Dead End Kids, and others. Along these lines, the "road shows" of Bing Crosby and Bob Hope started in the thirties. All these films have been called the forerunners of the modern television series.

Records and radio spawned phenomenal sales of sheet music with covers depicting a wealth of stars and scenes from their famous productions. These sheets provide enduring and endearing mementos of the songs, dances, and faces of films that helped America forget, if only for a few hours, its most trying of times. And these films and their music represent one of the greatest, most creative decades in movie history. These were the golden days of Hollywood, not to be seen again.

Except for a very few songs about the Great Depression, the popular music of the thirties, and especially that of the movie musicals, dealt mainly with personal issues, especially romance. Fantasy was what people wanted, and a sophisticated, witty, polished song genre that ignored the poor rural white or urban black was the result. It would remain for the later forties and fifties to add to this American product the music of protest, blues, and poverty, and thereby enrich the nation's growing musical melting pot.

"ALL THE THINGS YOU ARE"

The Forties

"This Is the Army"

WORLD WAR II

The 1940s ushered in an era of rapid movement for the United States, both socially and musically. Swing, with its catchy improvisations, was popular. The country danced its way through the numerous contortions of the jitterbug and the boogie-woogie. The Big Bands were still the rage with Glenn Miller's "Chattanooga Choo Choo" and Tommy Dorsey's "This Love of Mine" reaching the top of the charts. Eager listeners appreciated the intricate arrangements of instrumentalists with these bands as well as such featured vocalists as Ray Eberle, Perry Como, and Jo Stafford. The Andrews Sisters charmed the nation with their peppy hits like "Don't Sit Under the Apple Tree." It was in this musical atmosphere that America became a part of World War II.

Although a number of good musical films and individual songs were inspired by the war, there was nothing like the outpouring of song that occurred dur-

ing World War I. Americans were more jaded now. They had lived through the "war to end all wars," the decadent twenties, the sophisticated thirties, the Depression, and the outrage at the Nazi onslaughts. War could no longer be glorified with jingoistic slogans or softened with sentimentality. The younger generation was cynical and their elders were disillusioned by the fact that their sacrifices had not brought about the new world they had fought for. This was a troubled world that was brought ever closer together by expanding communications and travel technologies. War machines were more sophisticated. The world moved at a faster pace.

War songs were different, too. Now hundreds of

Above: Songs revealing patriotic sentiments helped sell war bonds.

Left: Vivian Blaine played a burlesque dancer who hits the big time in this 1945 musical whose only memorable tune was this Perry Como hit.

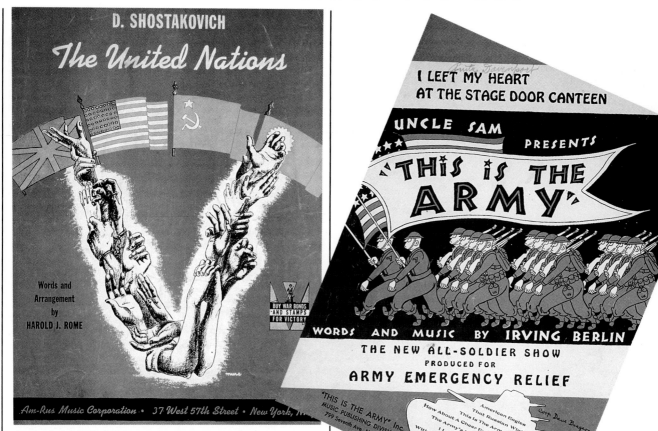

A song to cement Allied relations.

Irving Berlin's song
from his famous soldier show.

This expressionistic cover vividly portrays battle action in
World War II.

them were written, performed over the radio, and
forgotten. Radio unknowingly helped this to happen.
War was not glamorous. The grim daily news reports
brought this reality home to Americans as never before and encouraged them to forget the songs almost
as soon as they heard them.

However, World War II did give birth to some
memorable songs. Films such as *Hollywood Canteen,
Here Come the Waves,* and *Follow the Boys* contained
many wartime hits. The 1943 film *A Guy Named Joe*
had the hit song "I'll Get By," originally written in
1928, and *Thank Your Lucky Stars* of the same year
had "They're Either Too Young or Too Old," which
concerns itself with the wartime draft and the dearth
of available men. The tearjerker "I'll Walk Alone,"
introduced by Dinah Shore in 1944, was from the film
Follow the Boys, and the wishful "Say a Pray'r for the
Boys Over There" was featured in the film *Hers to
Hold. Here Come the Waves* featured Bing Crosby and
Betty Hutton in military uniforms on the sheet-music
covers.

Individual songs were written by some of America's

great song craftsmen to help the war effort. "Praise the Lord and Pass the Ammunition" was composed in 1942 by Frank Loesser after the Japanese attack on Pearl Harbor. It featured an interesting expressionistic cover and sold over 1 million copies of sheet music. Loesser also contributed "What Did You Do in the Infantry" in 1943 while he was in the service. "Comin' In on a Wing and a Prayer" (Adamson and McHugh) was introduced by Eddie Cantor. "G.I. Jive," with a wonderful cartoon cover of a soldier shirking KP to dance, was composed by Johnny Mercer, and Sammy Cahn and Jule Styne contributed "Vict'ry Polka." Other popular titles included "God Bless America," popularized by Kate Smith, and "There's a Star Spangled Banner Waving Somewhere."

Songs that spoke of other lands with empathy also became wartime hits. "The White Cliffs of Dover" and "Lili Marlene," among others, showed how world events were coming closer.

A lesser-known song sheet produced in 1942 was titled "The United Nations (On the March)." It exhorted the Allies to victory, and its cover pictured hands clasped in prayer and reaching upward toward their flags. The music was by the Russian composer Dimitry Shostakovich, the words were by Harold Rome, and it was produced by the Am-Rus Music Corp. Other Am-Rus editions included "(A New Hit Song from Our Soviet Ally) Sascha-Pascha-Yascha" and "Meadowland," which was featured in several films and reprinted in the *U.S. Army Hit Kit of Songs.* All sheets contained Russian as well as English words and bore the "Buy U.S. war bonds" stamp.

Cole Porter's "You'd Be So Nice to Come Home To" and Sammy Fain and Irving Kahal's "I'll Be Seeing You," recorded in 1944 by Frank Sinatra, were the quintessential "heartbreak of separation" love songs. They tenderly expressed the wartime longing and wistful hope that everyone would come home again.

"But Beautiful"

MOVIES

THE 1940s TURNED ANOTHER PAGE for the movies as it did for America. The country was pulling out of the Depression and mobilizing for war. There was a great surge of patriotic spirit, which would be necessary as the shadow of international conflict grew.

The outpouring of great songs in American films continued well into and through the end of the decade. The tradition of movie musicals, begun in the 1930s, continued, especially at M-G-M. *The Ziegfeld Follies, Yankee Doodle Dandy, Meet Me in St. Louis,* and *Cover Girl* are just a few of the quality products that were created during the war years.

The sadness and worry of conflict strengthened the appetite of those left behind for light, frothy entertainment. Movie musicals such as *For Me and My Gal* and *The Fleet's In* satisfied that hunger.

Big bands, a musical phenomenon of the 1930s and 1940s, were often either the focus of a film story or musically central to the plot. Paul Whiteman, Glenn Miller, and the Dorsey brothers, among others, appeared in movies or had films made about them. Tommy Dorsey's theme song, "I'm Gettin' Sentimental Over You," was used on the soundtrack of three

1940s films: *Keep 'Em Flying, DuBarry Was a Lady,* and *A Song Is Born.*

Musical biographies were popular. Chopin, Brahms, and Gershwin were among the composers depicted in such films as *A Song to Remember* (1945), *Song of Love* (1947), and *Rhapsody in Blue* (1945).

Nostalgic glimpses into the American past were real crowd pleasers. *Meet Me in St. Louis* (1944) returned to the early 1900s with Judy Garland singing the famous "Trolley Song." *Ziegfeld Follies* (1946) showed the great days of the follies onstage. *Coney Island* and *Sweet Rosie O'Grady,* both of 1943, returned to the simpler times of earlier decades. *State Fair* (1945) produced a beautiful Rodgers and Hammerstein score, including "It's a Grand Night for Singing" and "It Might as Well Be Spring."

Nostalgia went back a little further than a few decades with the popularity of the Western. Always a feature of films from the silents onward, Westerns reflected the growing optimism about national progress and pride in America's heritage that emerged after the Depression. The country enjoyed such favorites as *They Died with Their Boots On* (1941) with

A bevy of stars appeared in the Oscar-winning drama *The Razor's Edge*, which featured this song, *left*.

This light musical comedy, *right*, featured Sonja Henie as a war refugee and John Payne as her foster parent, traveling with the Glenn Miller band (1941).

This upbeat hit from 1941 was inspired by a Santa Catalina Island greeting (1941).

This story of a pioneer woman in the business world featured Betty Grable and a Gershwin score (1946).

The multitalented James Cagney starred in this patriotic musical flick (1942).

(1943), with the lively tunes of Irving Berlin, rallied pride in America.

Twentieth Century-Fox made famous its stars such as Betty Grable and Alice Faye, favorites with the army troops. Whether contemporary (*Pin Up Girl* of 1944) or nostalgic (*Coney Island* of 1943), Betty Grable wore costumes to show her legs—and the enlisted men loved her for it. She served as a symbol of pride in the all-American-girl-as-movie-star that provided yet another escape from the horrors of war.

Other movie musicals that showcased the superb development of the genre included M-G-M's *Anchors Aweigh* and *On the Town*, both starring the great Gene Kelly. The forties also produced some "lasts"—films that marked the end of an era. Reunited in 1949 after a ten-year hiatus, Fred Astaire and Ginger Rogers made their last film together, *The Barkleys of Broadway*. It contained a wonderful rendition of "They Can't Take That Away from Me," a song they had introduced in 1937.

Into the early 1950s, the greatness continued with such films as *An American in Paris* and the magical *Singin' in the Rain*. By the mid-1950s, however, original movie musicals were practically a thing of the past. People had lost interest. Escapism, no longer needed, was replaced with "issue" films. The older stars, essential to the oeuvre—Fred Astaire, Gene Kelly, Rita Hayworth, Ginger Rogers, Betty Grable—had all but disappeared. By the beginning of the 1960s, most musicals were filmed productions of original stage plays —*Carousel* (1956), *The Pajama Game* (1957), *South Pacific* (1958), *My Fair Lady* (1964). A natural ebb and flow of tastes and concerns—rock and folk grew as social issues became of paramount importance—signaled the end of fifteen years of movie musicals whose innovation and appeal have never been surpassed.

Important songs from the best musical craftsmen of the era continued to come out of the dramas, comedies, and other film types. Berlin gave us "White Christmas" from *Holiday Inn* (1942) as well as "Be Careful It's My Heart" and "Let's Start the New Year Right." Jerome Kern offered "The Last Time I Saw Paris" (*Lady Be Good*, 1941), "Dearly Beloved" and "I'm Old Fashioned" (*You Were Never Lovelier*, 1942), "Long Ago and Far Away" (*Cover Girl*, 1944), and

Erroll Flynn and *She Wore a Yellow Ribbon* (1949) with John Wayne.

Interest in exotic places developed, perhaps from the looking outward caused by war abroad or perhaps from a need for a temporary escape. *The Pirate* (1948) with Judy Garland and Gene Kelly, *The Sea Hawk* (1940) with Erroll Flynn, *Weekend in Havana* (1941) with Carmen Miranda and Cesar Romero, and the continuing road shows of Crosby and Hope reflected this trend. The passion for exotic places was never more evident than in *Casablanca*, with Humphrey Bogart and Ingrid Bergman, the 1942 film that is considered a classic today.

Patriotic movies such as *Yankee Doodle Dandy* (1942), with James Cagney and the wonderful music of George M. Cohan, as well as *This Is the Army*

"All Through the Day" (*Centennial Summer,* 1946).

Harold Arlen, many of whose songs are "bluesy" in feel, produced, with Johnny Mercer, "Blues in the Night" (1941), featured in the movie of the same name with a mostly black cast. Other Arlen and Mercer songs included "That Old Black Magic," "Happiness Is a Thing Called Joe" from *Cabin in the Sky,* "My Shining Hour" and "One for My Baby" (*The Sky's the Limit*), and "Ac-Cent-Tchu-Ate the Positive" (*Here Come the Waves*). Harry Warren and Johnny Mercer won an Academy Award in 1946 for "On the Atcheson, Topeka and the Santa Fe" from *The Harvey Girls,* and wrote the other eight songs from that Judy Garland film, which included "It's a Great Big World" and "Swing Your Partner." The solo Mercer song "I'm an Old Cowhand (from The Rio Grande)" was sung by Roy Rogers in the 1943 film *King of the Cowboys.* Mercer and Warren's "You Must Have Been a Beautiful Baby" was featured in the 1946 *Eddie Cantor Story* and sung in 1949 by Doris Day in *My Dream Is Yours.*

Other standards that came out of 1940s films include "How Little We Know" and "There Will Never Be Another You" (*Iceland*), "The More I See You" (*Diamond Horseshoe*), "It's a Most Unusual Day" (*A Date with Judy*), "Like Someone in Love" (*Belle of the Yukon*), "It Could Happen to You" (*And the Angels Sing*), "I'll Remember April" (*Ride 'Em Cowboy*), "Spring Will Be a Little Late This Year" (*Christmas Holiday*), "Laura" (from the movie of the same name), "You Make Me Feel So Young" (*Three Little Girls in Blue*), "Time After Time" (*It Happened in Brooklyn*), and "Buttons and Bows" (*The Paleface*).

Another change had taken place by the 1950s, however. Television had made its debut, and Americans fell in love with this little box that could entertain families in their very own living rooms. Hollywood producers would need to adapt their plans to compete with the revolutionary new medium. Whatever they did, however, movies would never again achieve the heights of those from the enchanting thirties and forties.

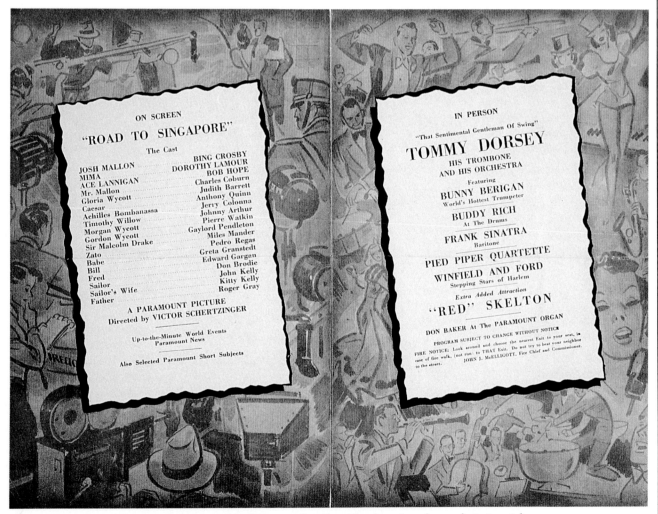

Gone are the days of the first-run movie and a big-name live show for the price of one admission ticket.

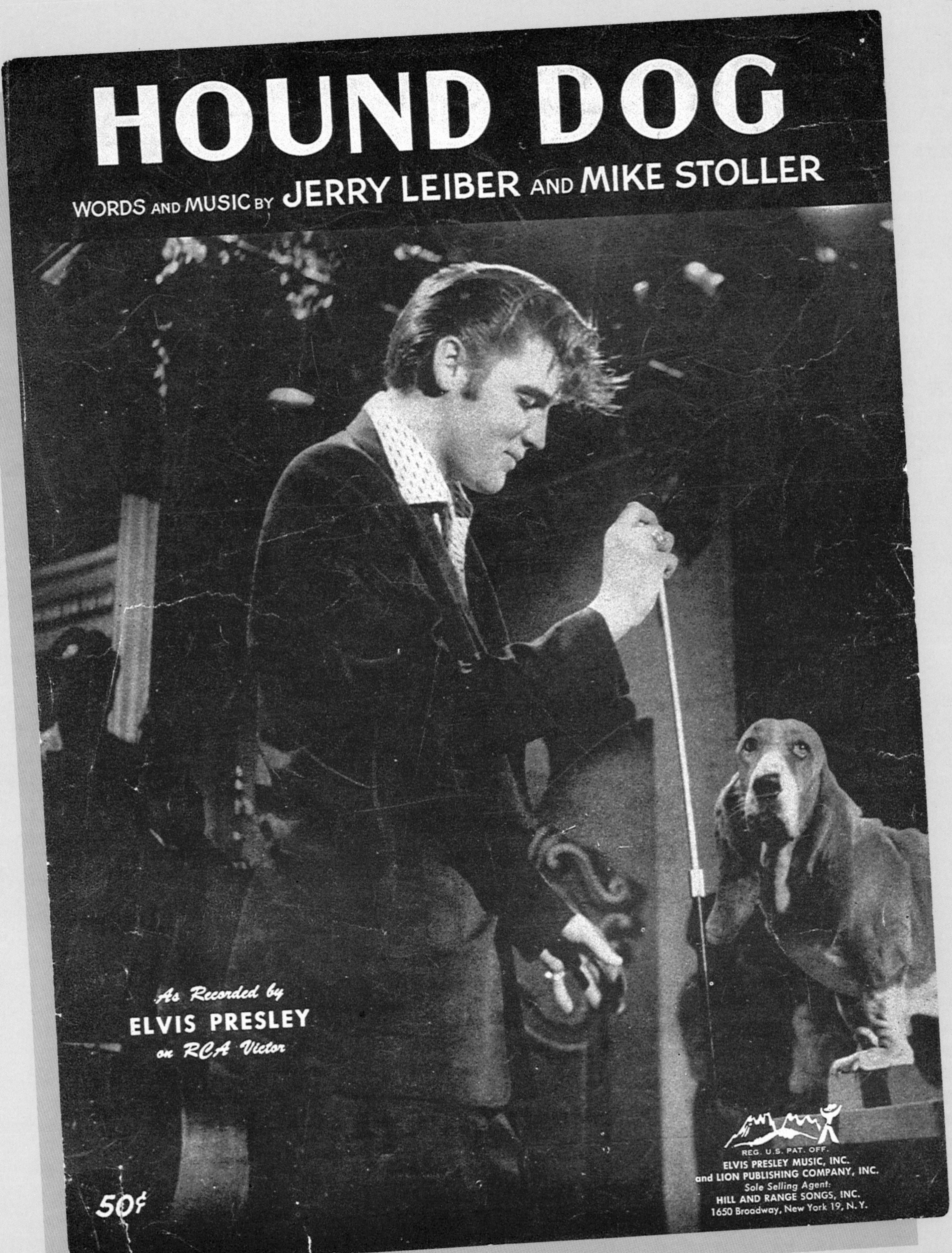
HOUND DOG
WORDS AND MUSIC BY JERRY LEIBER AND MIKE STOLLER
As Recorded by
ELVIS PRESLEY
on RCA Victor
50¢
REG. U.S. PAT. OFF.
ELVIS PRESLEY MUSIC, INC.
and LION PUBLISHING COMPANY, INC.
Sole Selling Agent:
HILL AND RANGE SONGS, INC.
1650 Broadway, New York 19, N.Y.

"THAT'LL BE THE DAY"

The Fifties and Beyond

"Love Me Tender"

ELVIS

Mention Elvis Presley and one pictures a gyrating, hip-swiveling, guitar-toting singer who took the country by storm in the 1950s with his unique rendition of such songs as "Hound Dog" and "Jailhouse Rock."

While Russian premier Nikita Khrushchev toured the West, superhighways superseded railroads, integration began to develop as a serious national force, and the world watched the wedding of film star Grace Kelly to Prince Rainier of Monaco, Elvis was managing to become a teen idol of monumental proportions as well as RCA's first artist to have two million-selling records in a row. Parents of the nation were horrified; they felt that this performer of pulsating rhythms and suggestive verses, with his outrageous movements and thuglike dress, was leading their children astray.

Elvis Presley, born and bred in the South, influenced by conventional gospel music as well as its Southern white adaptation and usurpation, transcended the form and remade it. While growing up he had become fluent in a number of black and white popular styles—country and western, blues, jazz, gospel. He did everything from playing the bass fiddle at the Grand Ole Opry to singing gospel with the Assembly of God church.

Despite early desires to become a professional gospel singer, Elvis began his career in 1954 as a rhythm and blues singer. How did he learn to sing "black"? By listening to black-only radio stations. Elvis listened closely and constantly to station WDIA in Memphis, where he heard the early work of such artists as Fats Domino, B. B. King, and Dinah Washington.

Elvis's first "hit" was recorded for Sun Records in 1954. His goal was to combine the feel of black music

Above: **Couples danced in strapless dresses and tuxedos to the strains of "Sea of Love" and "Sixteen Candles."**

Left: **In 1956, this was number 12 of the top fifty songs.**

• 1 1 9 •

with the audience appeal that could be created in the popular market by a white singer only. The songs "That's All Right Mama" and the white bluegrass "Blue Moon over Kentucky" did so.

The natural, innocent artifices of Elvis at the dawning of his career limn music history at the turn of the century and after. Syllabifying the words was an old practice going back to ragtime—for example, "If you lak-ah me like I lak-ah you" from "Under the Bamboo Tree." Elvis somehow managed to be both a throwback and on the cutting edge of a brand-new sound—rockabilly to rock-and-roll—by leaving the popular tune style that had dominated American music in the thirties and forties and going back to ragtime.

Although he had begun live performances and tours, radio was responsible for the singer's early success. Through 1954 and 1955, he recorded "I Love You Because," "Harbor Lights," and "Baby, Let's Play House" among others for Sun, and the radio exposure of these songs widened his fame. In February 1955, Elvis met Colonel Tom Parker, who would mastermind his career for the rest of his life. In August 1955, Elvis began breaking through the Mason-Dixon line. In July his "Baby, Let's Play House" had become his first record to appear on a national chart. By November, RCA completed negotiations and purchased his contract from Sun. And in January 1956, Elvis recorded his first megahit, "Heartbreak Hotel" (flip side, "I Got a Woman"). With his unique rendition of this and such other numbers as "Blue Suede Shoes," "Hound Dog," "Don't Be Cruel," "Treat Me Nice," "Love Me Tender," and "Teddy Bear," with their exaggerated emotionalism, threat of sexuality about to be unleashed, and a dollop of self-pity, Elvis guaranteed for himself a top spot in the annals of rock-and-roll history and the title of King of Rock-and-Roll.

His records were in such demand that his record company had to use the pressing facilities of competing manufacturers to meet its requirements. And his appearances on the "Ed Sullivan Show" caused a nationwide stir.

When Elvis returned from his hitch in the army in 1959, he came back to a changed and split rock-and-roll scene and the scandal of payola. He decided to align himself with traditional pop rather than with the new sound of soul. His recordings "It's Now or Never" and "Are You Lonesome Tonight?" sold 9 million and 5 million copies respectively.

In 1966, in an effort to prop up a now sagging career—Bob Dylan, the Beatles, and the Rolling Stones were raking in the millions—Elvis recorded a gospel album, "How Great Thou Art." Not only did it go gold, but it won a Grammy as best gospel album of the year. Later songs that were hits included "In the Ghetto" and "Suspicious Minds." Elvis had become a phenomenally successful live performer and continually broke audience records in Las Vegas. However, heavy addiction to drugs had taken its toll. For all he was paid, he ended up almost broke. Although his name was on the sheet music of "Heartbreak Hotel," "Don't Be Cruel," and "Love Me Tender," he never received a penny in broadcast composer royalties. Sycophants and hangers-on managed to dupe him out of money, and his own mental and physical illnesses combined to ensure his total inability to remain in control or understand his economic frailty.

Elvis Presley died on August 15, 1977. His funeral was a national event and his home still attracts hordes of visitors. His music remains today as quintessential "pure" rock-and-roll.

The right combination—an eclectic musician/performer, proper timing on the national front, and aggressive promotion in the new TV and more sophisticated radio and record industry—came together to make Elvis an unforgettable legend who lives on in memory, record, and song sheet. As John Lennon of the Beatles said, "Before Elvis, there was no one."

At the hop. The music world would soon change forever with the advent of the Beatles and the "psychedelic sixties."

"I'm a Believer"

POP, ROCK, FOLK, AND BEYOND

THE 1950s SEEMED A TIME OF PEACE and tranquility. World War II and the Korean conflict were over. Calm, reasonable war hero President Dwight David Eisenhower set a relaxed leadership tone for the country for eight years. Men were to get on about their business, button up their gray flannel suits, and storm the executive gates. Women, encouraged to leave their jobs in wartime factories, wore high heels and frilly aprons, baked cookies for the kids, and sent hubby off to work with a smile.

However, the Cold War had resulted in the Mc-Carthy witch hunts for Communists and subversives in government, racial unrest, and an American consciousness of inequality. "Separate but equal" became unconstitutional. Among the technological advances that developed after the war was the new entertainment gadget called television, and everyone had to have one.

Musically, America was at a fairly low ebb. The swing style of the Big Band Era was past, and popular music often dripped with sentimentality and curiously thin lyrics and melody. "Arrividerci, Roma," "Ghost Riders in the Sky," "Blue Velvet," "Doggie in the Window," and "Oh, My Pappa," are just a few examples of the vapidity that characterized popular music. Talented singers such as Peggy Lee, Frankie Laine, Perry Como, Rosemary Clooney, and Gogi Grant lent their talents to material that could not provide a message for the medium.

But in small towns, Southern hills, and urban centers, a new music form was ready to explode and change popular music forever. This was to be the music of youth—rock-and-roll. Its driving rhythms—good for dancing—bluesy structure, antiestablishment tone, and suggested sexuality burst into the consciousness of young men and women as "their" music. A restless youth culture that could not relate to its parents' music needed an anthem, and the potent mix of country and western and urban rhythm and blues provided it.

The words of many rock songs were less polished than songs of earlier decades. These lyrics came from writers without the sophisticated backgrounds of their previous counterparts. Disregarding the pat rhymes and smooth word combinations favored before, they poured into their lyrics basic emotion and raw experience.

By 1955, rock-and-roll had become known internationally. "Rock Around the Clock" by Bill Halley and the Comets achieved number-one status and was wildly popular in Europe, although in 1951, disc jockey Alan Freed, claiming to have coined the term *rock-and-roll*, had already brought black "race" records into white American consciousness. Toned-down rhythm and blues tunes such as "Chains of Love" by Joe Turner in 1951 and "Sh-Boom" by the Chords in 1954 were already popular with white youth. But the tremendous success of "Rock Around the Clock" made it clear that there was a real market for this kind of new music. Of the forty-two top songs counted by *Cashbox* in 1956, eighteen were rock-and-roll. Of the fifty top songs of 1957, rock-and-roll accounted for thirty-one.

With the discovery of Elvis Presley in 1956, the Everly Brothers—who patterned their style after black music—in 1957, and Buddy Holly's "That'll Be the Day" in 1957, the future of the new music was secure. Other extraordinarily high-selling hits that became classics in the early rock years included Little Richard's "Lucille"; Jerry Lee Lewis's "Whole Lotta

One of many popular groups
from the seventies with their hit love song.

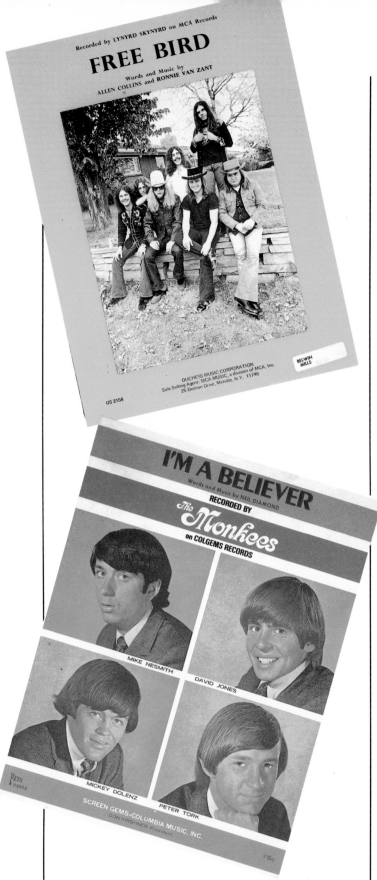

Top: One of the most enduring great rock songs. This sheet music may become more collectible due to the untimely accidental death of members of the band.

Above: The success of the Monkees was a result of the popularity of the Beatles. Note the haircuts on the cover of this Neil Diamond song.

Shakin' Goin' On"; the absurd "Rama Lama Ding Dong"; "Little Darlin'," with its ragtime-reminiscent syllabification; "A White Sport Coat" by Marty Robins and "I'm Walkin'" by Ricky Nelson—"wholesome" rock-and-roll; "Yakety Yak" by the Coasters; and "At the Hop" by Danny and the Juniors. Pop groups of the fifties, with their fresh brand of presentation, included the Charms, the Penguins, the Cadillacs, the Silhouettes, and the Drifters. Cleaned-up commercialized rock froth was represented by such teenage heartthrobs as Fabian and Bobby Rydell. By the end of the decade, rock music, once fresh and exciting, began to be overwhelmed by a steady flow of mediocrity. Except for the Beach Boys, a few novelty songs, and some good instrumentals, rock was foundering.

A new wave of music was to fill this temporary void. In 1958, the Kingston Trio's "Tom Dooley" reached number one on the charts. It was the first folk song to sell a million dollars' worth of records and it was the catalyst for a revival of folk music that dominated popular music for young and old until the emergence of the Beatles in 1964. From the Weavers and the Limeliters to Odetta to Peter, Paul, and Mary, from Harry Belafonte to Burl Ives, everyone was singing again.

Later into the sixties, folk music grew more serious and developed a political consciousness. For a while, it became the anthem for a generation who believed in civil rights, innovation, love and peace. Bob Dylan became its poet, Joan Baez its madonna, and Phil Ochs, among others, its philosopher.

The East and West coasts saw a split in the sixties. The East still loved Motown, soul, and its homegrown singers, but the West asserted its own unique personality with groups such as the Beach Boys and Jan and Dean who glorified the sun, the surf, and the speedy car.

The arrival of the Beatles in 1964 signaled a new wave of rock-and-roll innovation. They took America by storm with their number-one hit, "I Want to Hold Your Hand." Although the older generation was again somewhat put off by the group's "long" hair, unusual dress, and strong magnetism for the younger crowd, they had to acknowledge that the Beatles actually wrote melodies for their songs.

The Beatles produced scores of hits: "She Loves You," "Love Me Do," "Please, Please Me," "Do You Want to Know a Secret," and "Can't Buy Me Love," to name a few. Their English sound conquered America and was responsible for a wave of imitators. The British invasion included the Dave Clark Five, Gerry and the Pacemakers, Herman's Hermits, the Kinks,

and others. The Rolling Stones also hit the charts in 1964 for the first time, with "Not Fade Away."

Folk music became bitter, rock became psychedelic. Folk rock, a gentle, happy antidote to the anger of Dylan and the implied threat of the Rolling Stones, produced the Lovin' Spoonful, Sonny and Cher, the Turtles, the Mamas and the Papas, and the hugely talented Simon and Garfunkel. Modern soul music also began to thrive, and artists like Otis Redding, Wilson Pickett, Janis Joplin, and James Brown flourished. By the mid-1960s, folk music as an innovation faded. The art song as envisioned by Judy Collins and Joni Mitchell took its place. Flower children could listen to Jefferson Airplane, the Grateful Dead, Country Joe and the Fish, and the Doors.

Hard rock was represented by the Who, Cream, Iron Butterfly, Grand Funk Railroad, and Led Zeppelin with their emphasis on volume and action. Into the 1970s, we listened to Joe Cocker, Rod Stewart, Elton John, Carole King, and Creedence Clearwater Revival.

The phenomenon of rock video that began in 1978 changed popular music as much as rock-and-roll had done two decades earlier. Musicians now had to think about how they were perceived visually as well as aurally, and the visual presentation of a song became part of its art. Pop video stars like Bryan Adams, Air Supply, Pat Benatar, the Cars, Phil Collins, and Madonna, as well as country music singers and folk rockers, moved to create video accompaniments to their music.

From being an outlandish expression of teenage rebellion in the 1950s, rock music has come to dominate popular music. It is so diversified, its range so great, and its appeal so broad that, except in its most raucous heavy metal or punk style, it appeals to all generations and will probably continue to do so.

Of course, throughout this almost forty-year period there has always existed a body of purely commercial pop music that neither innovates nor follows, but instead ignores trends. Songs such as Frank Sinatra's "All the Way," Nat King Cole's "Mona Lisa," Peggy Lee's "Fever," and Engelbert Humperdinck's "Release Me" have marked no trends but continue to keep the sheet-music business, if not thriving, at least selling consistently. Standards such as "Up Where We Belong" from the movie *An Officer and a Gentleman* and "Truly" by Lionel Richie will surely be a part of the collectibles of the future. It seems difficult to imagine now, but someday collectors will treasure them as they do those sheets with stars Jenny Lind, Zip Coon, Fanny Brice, or Mary Pickford on the cover. They are the music history of the future.

"Everybody's Talkin'"

MISCELLANEOUS

THERE ARE LITERALLY HUNDREDS of categories of song sheets that either are becoming or will become collectibles. Many factors come into play in considering the potential value of such sheets, including personal interests and preferences. There are, however, a few categories to begin considering while obtaining pieces for a collection.

Special events that have happened recently might have song sheets connected with them that will increase in value. The Statue of Liberty's hundredth birthday is an example. Sheets commemorating the 1986 celebration are sure to command collectors' interest in the future.

Social and political statements as seen through song will become tomorrow's mirrors of history. Songs about political figures and special-interest groups are worth tucking away as valuable future memorabilia.

War has always engendered a proliferation of patriotic and sentimental sheet music. The Vietnam experience, however, resulted in a division of belief in the country that has only recently begun to heal. This divisiveness was reflected in a number of songs. The antiwar movement expressed its feelings in songs such as "Won't Get Fooled Again" (rock), "Talking Vietnam Pot-Luck Blues" (folk), and "Universal Soldier" (folk-rock). Country music, on the other hand, defended the war in Southeast Asia and criticized the peace and resistance movement and its adherents. Songs such as "Ballad of the Green Berets," "Okie from Muskogee," and "The Minute Men (Are Turning in Their Graves)" reflected those feelings.

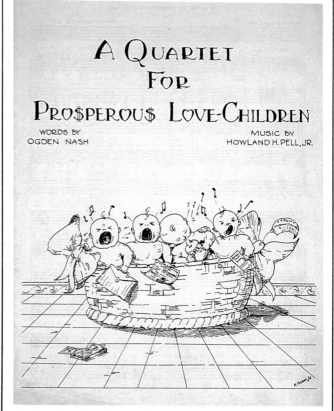

A privately printed song, discovered by the authors at a Connecticut estate sale, scathingly ridiculed United States political leadership in the forties. The words were by Ogden Nash and the music by Howland H. Pell, Jr.

Movie and theater music will probably always continue to be a sound addition to any collection. As particular shows, films, and stars are looked back

An especially beautiful lithograph of New York harbor adorns the cover of this song, written in 1885 to honor the gift of the Statue of Liberty by France to the United States.

Of the many country and western stars featured on the covers of sheet music, Tex Ritter, *right,* was an all-time favorite.

upon with nostalgia, their related sheet music is sure to become prized. Musical themes from popular television programs also fall into this category.

Country music is the music of "ordinary folks." Its commercial success suggests, however, that "ordinary folks" make up an awfully large portion of the populace. Whether Western style, bluegrass, urban country, or Deep South, country music owes its existence to the English-Irish-Scottish balladry that traveled to America in the 1700s and settled first in the Southeast. Western country is an amalgam of that tradition melded with evocative instrumentals from south of the border. Cajun fiddling from Louisiana lends its own distinct sound, and Southwest country is all of the traditions combined with an added fillip of mournful cowboy songs. Performers such as Tex Ritter, Ernest Tubb, Jimmie Rodgers, the Carter Family,

Willie Nelson, and Loretta Lynn are a very few among many who have been pictured on country music sheets.

Sheet music that defines a particular locale—"By the Time I Get to Phoenix," "New York, New York," "Galveston"—will always evoke interest, especially if the cover portrays the place as well as the singer. Songs about local landmarks, rivers, and buildings also fall into this category.

Sheets published privately (self-published) in limited editions are always of interest and can be ex-

LOOKOUT MOUNTAIN
WORDS BY
JOE GOODWIN
MUSIC BY
HALSEY K. MOHR
HOWARD AND HURST
Published by
Shapiro, Bernstein & Co.
MUSIC PUBLISHERS
224 West 47TH Street
New York
DUNK, N.Y.
5

This 1921 cover was taken from a magazine illustration by the famous Hamilton King.

This 1911 cover is a good example of the work of E. Pfeiffer.

Left: There was probably a song written for every state in the union. One from 1917 honors Tennessee.

Hurrah for Bushwick High

Words and Music
by
Rose Meisenhelder

This privately published song of 1912 was written to honor a Brooklyn, N.Y., high school that is still in existence.

pected to rise in value. At the very least, they give a clue to the continued entrepreneurship alive in this country. Examples are "The Jumping Frog of Calaveras," published in San Andreas, California, and retelling the famous short story by Mark Twain; "They Didn't Go Back On Uncle Sam," written and published by William H. Hyde, a Civil War veteran from New Jersey; and "Imperial Potentate March," written by Masonic leader Custis N. Guttenberger and distributed by a music store in Macon, Georgia.

Sheet-music covers from early animated films that featured cartoon characters on the covers are coveted. Collectors who specialize in Disneyana search avidly for all the sheets with songs from such movies as *Snow White and the Seven Dwarfs, Pinocchio, Bambi, The Three Little Pigs, Cinderella, Mary Poppins,* and *Song of the South.* As Disney developed material for television, song sheets featured such well-known figures as Davy Crockett (Fess Parker in a coonskin hat) and Johnny Tremain.

No matter what trends ultimately develop in sheet-music collecting, any purchase or find will be of high worth if you enjoy it. What seems ordinary today will seem laughable in twenty-five years, extraordinary in fifty, and unbelievable in seventy-five, and the pleasure that your collection brings—especially as a historical barometer—will be priceless.

"Paint Your Wagon"

ARTISTS AND LITHOGRAPHERS

SOME PEOPLE FALL IN LOVE with old sheet music because it is the history of the American people told in song, some lose their hearts to the music itself, but most of us probably treasure song sheets because of their covers. Simple or ornate, black-and-white or colored, done by a famous artist or an obscure house illustrator, they are the tantalizing bait that hooks new collectors and keeps them searching for "just one more" old house sale or bidding at just one more auction.

The history of very early sheet-music covers is thoroughly intertwined with that of its publishers and of American printmaking. Many famous names in lithography, such as Endicott, Jewett, Shaw, Sarony, and P. S. Duval, to mention a very few, printed sheet music from the late eighteenth until the late nine-

teenth century. Stables of artists who worked for the lithographers were less well known and collectors today are often not familiar with names such as John H. Bufford, W. K. Hewitt, or C. E. Lewis, although they were fine artists.

Music illustration up to about 1820 or so usually consisted of fancy capital letters, calligraphic titles, or small vignettes engraved below the title on the first page of music. Later, some sheet music had both a pictorial title page and caption title vignettes. According to David Tatham, between 1820 and 1870 publishers, interested in selling more and more sheet music to a public now clamoring for it, gave ever-

Right: **Norman Rockwell's well-known cover illustration from *Life* magazine done in 1918.**

Your Song—My Song—Our Boys' Song

OVER THERE

WORDS AND MUSIC BY
GEORGE M. COHAN

POPULAR · EDITION
LEO. FEIST INC. NEW YORK
HERMAN DAREWSKI MUSIC PUBLISHING CO. LONDON, ENG.

NATIVE·HAWAIIAN·SONGS·FROM

OLIVER·MOROSCO'S·PRODUCTION

THE BIRD OF PARADISE

BY
RICHARD·WALTON·TULLY

FAREWELL (Aloha Oe) 60
BURNING LOVE (Ahi Wela) . . .50
FORGET ME NOT (Mai Poina Oe) .50
HAWAIIAN HULA (Instrumental) .60
WALTZES 60

JOHN·FRANKLIN·MUSIC·Co······NEW·YORK

Right: A stunningly designed Art Nouveau–reminiscent cover from 1915.

THE JAPANESE SANDMAN SONG

TOLD BY
RAYMOND B. EGAN
SET TO MUSIC BY
RICHARD A. WHITING

6

JEROME H. REMICK & CO.
NEW YORK
DETROIT

Gene Buck, the prolific songwriter, illustrator, and past president of ASCAP, created this exotic cover in 1912.

From 1920, a typical Frederick Manning cover—a lovely woman done in soft-edged pastel tones.

A striking patriotic cover done by Starmer in 1911.

growing space and importance to the illustrated title page. As years passed, the vignette became larger and took up more space on the title page until it finally took the form we are more familiar with today—the single large illustration including title, lettering, and music information.

When lithographic printing became available in America, it further broadened the scope of illustrative possibilities. Less expensive and time-consuming for the publisher than engraving, it allowed the artist to create his own design and ensure its reproduction as he wanted it, bypassing the engraver's hand. After 1830 most title pages were lithographed, and the reduction in cost allowed music to be published for all occasions, public and private.

Major illustrators of early sheet music included David Claypoole Johnston, Robert Cooke, Charles Parsons, William Rimmer, and George Loring. Color printing—unlike hand-tinting, which was in use in the early nineteenth century—was initially very expensive and difficult to master. After about 1850, however, it reached its zenith and continued to be a desirable way to enhance the sales of less-than-enchanting music.

In the early years of their developing skills, artists who were to become well-known painters occasionally illustrated sheet music. Such individuals included Winslow Homer (for Bufford Publishing, "The Ratcatchers Daughter," "Polka Mazurkas," and "The Wheelbarrow Polka"), James Abbott McNeill Whistler (1852), Thomas Nast ("The Celebrated Arion

Music was often engraved while the cover was produced using the newer method of lithography, as is the case in this charming cover (c. 1840) from the fine lithographer P. S. Duval.

This beautifully rendered lithograph was done by Sarony and Major in 1851.

Fancy lettering and calligraphic titles were used on early sheet music before the development of the pictorial title page.

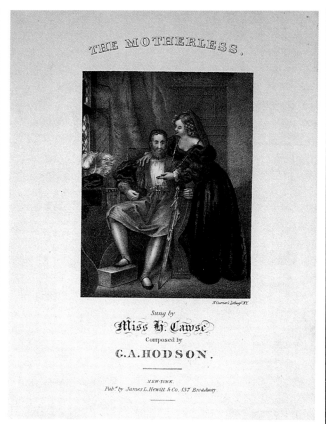

A Nathaniel Currier lithograph decorates the cover of a mid-nineteenth-century sheet.

Carnival Festival March 1867"), and Nathaniel Currier of Currier and Ives.

Toward the end of the nineteenth century, photographic printing replaced lithography. Cheap and easy to reproduce, it transformed the business of sheet-music illustration once again. Cover designs representing art trends—Art Nouveau, cubism, expressionism, Art Deco—were often created by more ambitious cover artists whose designs sometimes surpassed the artwork itself. Photographs of performers became popular in the 1890s. Their artistic integration into the cover design, when well done, could be quite alluring. In any case, it has provided collectors with a wonderful history of the stars of vaudeville, early theater, and the silver screen.

Better-known, more recent sheet-music artists include Starmer, who practiced from the 1890s to World War II; Albert Barbelle; Gene Buck, also a well-known lyricist and former president of ASCAP; Frederick S. Manning, known for his rendering of beautiful women; Andre DeTakacs, master of many styles; E. L. Pfeiffer; John Frew; Pud Lane; and Wohlman. One artist signed her covers with only R.S. or a stylized rose; her identity remains an intriguing mystery. Others included Leff, a wonderful Art Deco designer; Politzer; Edgar Keller; S. Knox; Armstrong, another creator of beautiful women; and Hirt, whose covers also often featured lovely girls. As in the nineteenth century, a few famous artists loaned their talent to sheet-music illustration. These included the illustrator Hamilton King; Norman Rockwell ("Over There," "Little Grey Mother of Mine," "Down Where the Lilies Grow," and "Lady Bird Cha Cha Cha"); James Montgomery Flagg; and Albert Vargas of pin-up girl fame.

Eventually, photographs of stars took up more and more cover space, leaving the artist little opportunity for expression. Covers from the 1930s and 1940s showed this trend.

Sheet-music illustration as an art form had died. With the development of radio and television, the need for printed music had diminished. Music illustration now began to be concentrated in poster design and innovative and beautiful artwork for record album covers, mostly of rock music. Early examples of these illustrations are now coveted by collectors, and will undoubtedly increase in value. In the meantime, the legacy left to us on the sheet-music covers of the past two hundred years is an enduring one and a clear mirror of the past.

WHEN OLD BILL BAILEY
PLAYS THE UKALELE
WORDS and MUSIC BY
CHAS. McCARRON
AND
NAT. VINCENT
BROADWAY MUSIC CORPORATION
WILL VON TILZER PRESIDENT
145 WEST 45TH ST NEW YORK
14 MONMOUTH STREET,
RED BANK, N. J.

Hirt's impressive, colorful paintings of beautiful women are represented on the cover of a 1908 Kerry Mills song.

Cartoon covers are hard to come by. This one, featuring the famous syndicated characters Mutt and Jeff (1911), is an outstanding example.

Left: Andre DeTakacs, a prolific illustrator able to adapt to many different styles, did this appealing cover in 1915.

"TILL WE MEET AGAIN"

Afterword

Music was, is, and will continue to be the heartbeat of a nation. Whether large or small, in war or peace, highly developed or third world, every country has its own voice, the one given it by its people.

America is no different. For 250 years, it has sung its heart out in church, at home, on the stage, out on the range, in the barroom, and around the parlor piano. Through the skills of a thousand songsters, it has wept for its dead, cheered its heroes, praised its leaders, and ridiculed its foes.

Our American sheet music is a truly remarkable combination of the artistic merits of its covers, the lasting record of the songs within these covers, and,

as a whole, a reflection of the country's colorful history.

To play and sing the songs while treasuring the beauty of their covers is a rich and wonderful pastime.

And to those who revel in the pleasure of collecting the many masterpieces, everyday items, oddities, and rarities, may there be everlasting joys and personal rewards in this unique way of preserving enchanting remnants of America's heritage. For we still go on much as we did a hundred years ago—optimistically, hopefully, and steadfastly, and with a song in our hearts.

"HOW AM I TO KNOW?"

Collectors' Guide

"Among My Souvenirs"

EVALUATING SHEET CONDITION

Sheet music is, by its very nature, fragile—meant to be used or even abused, enjoyed until its style or subject passes from popularity, then thrown away in favor of a new, revised, more popular edition. It is a miracle that any of it survives.

Evaluating the condition of a sheet must take into consideration its age and rarity. Surprisingly, the older sheets, those from 100 to 150 years ago, are usually in better shape than those printed around or after the turn of the century. The reason for this is that the mass production of paper, which began during the Industrial Revolution, changed the traditional chemistry of paper. A shortage of rags, the fibers of which all early paper was made from, forced paper makers to use wood pulp, which was then treated with an alum-rosin compound to make the paper smoother. The compound, however, eventually broke down into acids that ate the wood-pulp fibers. So a copy of "Farewell Awhile My Native Isle" from 1840 may be as perfect as the day it was purchased, while your prized copy of "Over There" may eventually crumble before your eyes.

In the meantime, as collectors endeavor to save and protect as much history as possible in music, there are a number of factors that come into play when evaluating the worth of a particular sheet-music item—whether for the purpose of buying, selling, or keeping it.

Collecting experience will in itself help you develop a fine sense of what is or is not a desirable piece. In addition, keep the following factors in mind.

RARITY OF SHEET/DEMAND ON OPEN MARKET

Attendance at music collectors' club meetings, reading related articles and books, talking with other collectors, scanning auction lists, shopping at antiques sales, and so forth, will develop a good sense of what is rare and what is not.

Even a poor copy of an unusual Stephen Foster item will be of monetary worth. On the other hand, a poor copy of E. T. Paull's "Burning of Rome" will not be of as much value since there are still good copies around.

Certain composers or types of covers are in greater demand at one time or another by collectors. It is good to keep aware of these trends in case an opportunity arises to buy or sell.

TYPE AND AMOUNT OF DAMAGE

A copy of any sheet music, old or new, that is found in perfect condition is most unusual. Consequently, there is a wide curve of variables, short of perfect, that have an effect on the ultimate value of a given sheet. Some guidelines for determining the value are:

MINT
- Music store condition
- No stamped or written names, tears, dirt, smears, frays, etc.

GOOD
- Cover separated from spine
- Ink or pencil signatures
- Music store stamp

Unless it is a phenomenally rare item, the more serious the damage and the more different categories of damage that a sheet possesses, the more worthless it will be. A folded sheet with severe water damage, for example, would fit this category. However, a neat pencil signature and a small tear cannot destroy a worthwhile and valuable sheet.

Some early music (pre-1870) was bound—sewn by thread—into books. This does not detract from the condition as long as the sheets were not torn during removal. Small holes from thread along the left side of very old music should thus not detract from its value. The same is not true, however, for trimmed music. Usually older music, it was cut to fit into more modern-size piano benches or cabinets. This detracts seriously from the value of the sheets, which are now useful mainly as a record of the music itself.

If any sheet is in terrible condition—unless of course you need it for musical purposes, or it is an extraordinarily rare piece of historical Americana, or you have a strong personal interest—wait until another, choicer copy comes along. Your collection will be the better for it.

"Button Up Your Overcoat"

CARE AND MAINTENANCE

The value of a collection of sheet music can grow or diminish noticeably as a result of the quality of care it is given.

Sheets that are exposed to excesses of moisture and temperature, are carelessly stored and handled, or are hastily and thoughtlessly repaired are permanently decreased in beauty and value. As old sheets become rarer and, at the same time, in greater demand, it is imperative for the collector to become more sensitive to the requirements of caring for such treasures.

Certain basic guidelines should be followed to maintain a collection.

STORAGE

- Keep sheets *flat*. Stack your music. Standing it upright will eventually cause fraying and creasing of edges.
- *Encase* them in clear plastic polyester Mylar sheets to prevent sticking and to minimize the negative effects of handling.
- Keep them as *dust-free* as possible. Libraries often use acid-free boxes to stack music in, which may be slid in and out for use or display. They are ideal but do take up space.
- Keep sheets in *cool temperatures* and in *low humidity*. Every extra five degrees of cold doubles the life of paper.

CLEANING

- Wipe sheets *gently* with a soft, dry cloth to remove surface dirt.
- Remove soiled borders and pencil signatures *carefully*, with an art gum eraser. This applies only to old, high-rag-content sheets.
- *Never* attempt to wash a print with any hand-painting on the cover. This should be done by an expert.
- Extremely filthy prints, usually pre-1870 engraved or lithographed sheets with high rag content, may be washed in clear, warm, gently running water for approximately ten minutes. Blot dry, place between two pieces of blotting paper, clamp between two sheets of plywood, and leave to dry for several days.

REPAIR

- Use Booksaver glue to repair—only on old, high-rag-content sheets.
- Do repairs on wax-paper surfaces.
- *Never* use cellophane tape—only archival repair tape.
- Cover repairs with wax paper, weight with books, and leave for three to six hours.

If, horror of horrors, you insist upon keeping sheet music in a basement and it floods—say good-bye to the later sheets. They will be beyond repair. But in case of water damage, early rag prints may be saved. Freeze-dry them immediately to prevent mildew and minimize damage. If you have no freezer large enough, sprinkle cornstarch between the pages. After a few days of drying with pages loosely separated, brush the cornstarch off and dry the pages carefully with an electric heater lamp.

Repairs for rare music may be performed with rice paper and wheat paste, but this is a delicate and tedious process. For those sheets that are considerably rare and valuable, it is worth the money to go to a professional print restorer who can clean and repair the piece as well as remove brown spots (foxing) caused by fungus.

FRAMING

- Never cut sheets to frame size, or separate the cover from the rest of the music.
- Make the package as airtight as possible. Tape a rag-content mat and backboard along with the print and glass on all four sides before putting into the frame.
- If you have sheets professionally framed, be sure to tell the framer to use acid-free materials.
- Glue brown paper, cut to size, to the back of the frame for added protection.
- Do not hang the framed sheet music in sunlight. It will fade the print.

SOURCES FOR CARE OF EPHEMERA

For archival polyester plastic envelopes and archival mending tape:

University Products, Inc.
P.O. Box 101
South Canal St.
Holyoke, MA 10141

Conservation Resources International
1111 North Royal St.
Alexandria, VA 22314

Specialists in conservation and restoration:

Madeline Braun
(212) 989-6279 (by appointment only)
Cleaning, restoring, and repairing

Carolyn Horton & Associates, Inc.
(212) 989-1471 (by appointment only)
Conservation of all works on paper

For plastic sheet-music covers:

MARSCO
1713 Central St.
Evanston, IL 60201

"Ask Anyone Who Knows"

MAJOR COLLECTIONS

The following partial listing will aid the reader in further research and study of American sheet music.

MUSEUMS

Maryland Historical Society (Baltimore)
Museum of the City of New York
New-York Historical Society (New York City)

LIBRARIES

Bagaduce Music Lending Library (Blue Hill, ME)
Chicago Public Library, Music Section
Erie County Public Library, Music Department (Buffalo, NY)
Library of Congress (Washington, DC)
Metropolitan Toronto (Canada) Library
National Library of Ottawa (Canada)
Newberry Library (Chicago)
The New York Public Library, Library and Museum of the Performing Arts at Lincoln Center

UNIVERSITIES

Baylor University (Waco, TX)
Brigham Young University (Provo, UT)
Brooklyn College of the City University of New York, Institute for the Study of American Music
Brown University (Providence, RI), Harris Collection at John Hay Library

Columbia University (New York City)
Indiana University, Lilly Library, Bloomington
Johns Hopkins University (Baltimore, MD), Milton S. Eisenhower Library, Lester S. Levy Special Collection
Trinity College (Hartford, CT)
University of California at Los Angeles, Music Library Archive of Popular Music
University of Illinois—Urbana
University of Michigan (Ann Arbor)
University of Oklahoma at Norman
University of Pittsburgh (PA), Foster Hall Collection of the Stephen Foster Memorial
University of South Dakota at Vermillion, Shrine to Music Museum and Center for the Study of the History of Musical Instruments
University of Toronto (Canada)
Yale University (New Haven, CT)

ADDITIONAL RESOURCES

American Antiquarian Society, 185 Salisbury Street, Worcester, MA 01609
American Society of Composers, Authors and Publishers (ASCAP), 1 Lincoln Plaza, New York, NY 10023
Broadcast, Music, Inc. (BMI), 320 West 57th Street, New York, NY 10019
Sonneck Society for American Music and Music in America (newsletter), 14–34 155th Street, Whitestone, NY 11357

"Hail, Hail, the Gang's All Here"

CLUBS

Clubs for sheet-music collectors include:

City of Roses Sheet Music Collectors Club
43125 East Flavel
Portland, OR 97220

National Sheet Music Society
1597 Fair Park Ave.
Los Angeles, CA 90041
(newsletter; contact for local chapter information)

New York Sheet Music Society
P.O. Box 1126
East Orange, NJ 07019
(newsletter)

Publications of interest to collectors are:

Keyboard Classics
352 Evelyn Street
Paramus, NJ 07653-0933

Ragtime Society
P.O. Box 520, Station A
Weston, Ontario, Canada M9N 3N3

Remember That Song
5821 N. 67th Ave., Suite 103–306
Glendale, AZ 85311

Sheet Music Exchange
P.O. Box 69
Quicksburg, VA 22847

Sheet Music Magazine
352 Evelyn Street
Paramus, NJ 07653-0933

Adams, Mildred. *The Right to Be People.* J. B. Lippincott Co., 1967.

The American Animated Cartoon: A Critical Anthology. Edited by Danny and Gerald Peary. New York: E.P. Dutton, 1980.

The American Heritage History of World War I. By the editors of American Heritage. New York: American Heritage Publishing Co., 1964.

The American Heritage Songbook. Compiled and arranged by Ruth and Norman Lloyd. New York: American Heritage Publishing Co., 1969.

Atkinson, Brooks. *Broadway.* New York: Macmillan Publishing Co., 1974.

Austin, William W. *"Susanna," "Jeanie," and "The Old Folks at Home": The Songs of Stephen C. Foster from His Time to Ours.* New York: Macmillan Publishing Co., 1975.

Bazelon, Irwin. *Knowing the Score: Notes on Film Music.* New York: Arco Publishing, 1975.

Berlin, Edward A. *Reflections and Research on Ragtime.* I.S.A.M. Monograph #24, Institute for Studies in American Music. Conservatory of Music, Brooklyn College of the City University of New York, 1987.

The Bicentennial Collection of American Music. Volume I, 1698–1800. Carol Stream, Ill.: Hope Publishing Co., 1974.

Blesh, Rudi. "Scott Joplin: Black-American Classicist." In *Scott Joplin: Collected Piano Works,* edited by Vera Brodsky Lawrence. The New York Public Library, 1971.

Brand, Oscar. *Songs of 76: Folksinger's History of the Revolution.* New York: M. Evans and Company, 1972.

Brown, William W. "The Anti-Slavery Harp." Boston, 1848. From the Drury College Library through the auspices of Dr. S. R. Wagner.

Brownlow, Kevin. *The Parade's Gone By.* New York: Ballantine Books, 1968.

Burton, Jack. *The Tin Pan Alley Blue Book.* Vol. I. Watkins Glen, N.Y.: Century House, 1962.

Chase, Gilbert. *America's Music: From the Pilgrims to the Present.* New York: McGraw-Hill Book Co., 1955.

Cook, David A. *A History of Narrative Film.* New York: W. W. Norton & Co., 1981.

Croce, Arlene. *The Fred Astaire and Ginger Rogers Book.* New York: Outerbridge & Lazard, 1972.

Dichter, Harry, and Elliot Shapiro. *Handbook of Early American Sheet Music 1768–1889.* New York: Dover Books, 1977.

Earley, Steven C. *An Introduction to American Movies.* New York: New American Library, 1978.

Elson, Louis C. *The National Music of America and Its Sources.* Boston: L. C. Page & Company, 1924.

Engel, Lehman. *The American Musical Theater.* New York: Macmillan Publishing Co., 1975.

Ewen, David. *Complete Book of the American Musical Theater.* New York: Henry Holt and Company, 1958.

———. *Great Men of American Popular Song.* Englewood Cliffs, N.J.: Prentice-Hall, 1970.

———. *The Life & Death of Tin Pan Alley: The Golden Age of American Popular Music.* New York: Funk & Wagnalls Co., 1964.

———. *Panorama of American Popular Music.* Englewood Cliffs, N.J.: Prentice-Hall, 1957.

———. *The Story of America's Musical Theater.* Philadelphia: Chilton Book Co., 1961.

Fenin, George N., and William K. Everson. *The Western: From Silents to Seventies.* New York: Penguin Books, 1973.

Forma, Warren. *They Were Ragtime.* New York: Grosset & Dunlop, 1976.

Franklin, Joe. *Classics of the Silent Screen.* Secaucus, N.J.: The Citadel Press, 1959.

Freeman, Larry. *The Melodies Linger On: 50 Years of Popular Song.* Watkins Glen, N.Y.: Century House, 1951.

Gammond, Peter. *Scott Joplin and the Ragtime Era.* New York: St. Martin's Press, 1975.

The Gold of Rock & Roll 1955–1967. Edited by H. Kandy Rohde. New York: Arbor House, 1970.

Goldberg, Isaac. *Tin Pan Alley: A Chronicle of the American Popular Sheet Music Racket.* New York: The John Day Co., 1930.

Gray, Andy. *Great Pop Stars.* London: Hamlyn, 1973.

Green, Stanley. *Encyclopedia of the Musical Film.* New York: Oxford University Press, 1981.

———. *Ring Bells! Sing Songs! Broadway Musicals of the 1930's.* New York: Galahad Books, 1971.

Greenway, John. *American Folksongs of Protest.* New York: Octagon Books, 1971.

Griffith, Elisabeth. *In Her Own Right: The Life of Elizabeth Cady Stanton.* New York: Oxford University Press, 1984.

Halliwell, Leslie. *The Filmgoer's Companion.* New York: Avon Books, 1978.

Hamm, Charles. *Yesterdays: Popular Song in America.* New York: W. W. Norton & Co., 1979.

Hancock, Nancy Knox. "The Myth of Seneca Falls: A New Look at American Feminism 1831–1861." Unpublished thesis, Mount Holyoke College, 1973.

Harris, Charles K. *After the Ball: Forty Years of Melody.* New York: Frank-Maurice, 1926.

Heaps, Willard A. and Porter. *The Singing Sixties: The Spirit of the Civil War Days Drawn from the Music of the Times.* Norman: University of Oklahoma Press, 1960.

Henderson, Mary C. *Theater in America.* New York: Harry N. Abrams, 1986.

Higham, Charles. *The Art of the American Film.* Garden City, N.Y.: Anchor Press, 1974.

Hirschhorn, Clive. *The Warner Bros. Story.* New York: Crown Publishers, 1979.

Hitchcock, N. Wiley. *Music in the United States: A Historical Introduction.* Englewood Cliffs, N.J.: Prentice-Hall, 1969.

Hoogerwerf, Frank W. *Confederate Sheet-Music Imprints.* Brooklyn College of the City University of New

York, Institute for Studies in American Music, 1984.

Howard, John Tasker. *Our American Music: A Comprehensive History from 1620 to the Present.* New York: Thomas Y. Crowell Co., 1965.

————. *Stephen Foster: America's Troubadour.* New York: Thomas Y. Crowell Co., 1934.

Howard, John Tasker, and George Kent Bellows. *A Short History of Music in America.* New York: Thomas Y. Crowell Co., 1957.

Jackson, George Stuyvesant. *Early Songs of Uncle Sam.* Boston: Bruce Humphries, 1933.

Jacobs, Lewis. *The Rise of the American Film.* New York: Teachers College Press, 1967.

Jahn, Mike. *The Story of Rock: From Elvis Presley to the Rolling Stones.* New York: Quadrangle, 1973.

Jasen, David A., and Trebor Jay Tichenor. *Rags & Ragtime: A Musical History.* New York: The Seabury Press, 1978.

Kahn, E.J., Jr. *The Merry Partners: The Age and Stage of Harrigan and Hart.* New York: Random House, 1955.

Kaminsky, Stuart M. *American Film Genres: Approaches to a Critical Theory of Popular Film.* New York: Dell Publishing Co., 1974.

Katz, Ephraim. *The Film Encyclopedia.* New York: Perigee Books, 1979.

Kaufmann, Helen L. *From Jehovah to Jazz.* Freeport, N.Y.: Books for Libraries Press, 1968.

Kinney, Troy, and Margaret West. *The Dance: Its Place in Art and Life.* New York: Frederick A. Stokes Co., 1914.

Klamkin, Marian. *Old Sheet Music: A Pictorial History.* New York: Hawthorn Books, 1975.

Kobal, John. *A History of Movie Musicals: Gotta Sing, Gotta Dance.* New York: Exeter Books, 1983.

Latham, David. *The Lure of the Striped Pig: The Illustration of Popular Music in America 1820–1870.* Barre, Mass.: Imprint Society, 1973.

Laufe, Abe. *Broadway's Greatest Musicals.* New York: Funk & Wagnalls Co., 1977.

Lawrence, Vera Brodsky. *Music for Patriots, Politicians, and Presidents: Harmonies and Discords of the First Hundred Years.* New York: Macmillan Publishing Co., 1975.

Lawton, Richard. *A World of Movies.*

New York: Dell Publishing Co., 1974.

Levy, Lester S., *Give Me Yesterday: American History in Song, 1890–1920.* Norman: University of Oklahoma Press, 1975.

————. *Grace Notes in American History: Popular Sheet Music from 1820 to 1900.* Norman: University of Oklahoma Press, 1967.

————. *Picture the Songs.* Baltimore: The Johns Hopkins University Press, 1976.

Lewine, Richard, and Alfred Simon. *Songs of the American Theater.* New York: Dodd, Mead & Co., 1973.

Lindeman, Carolynn A. "Women in Rags," *Keyboard Classics Magazine,* July/August 1985.

Lovell, John, Jr. *Black Song: The Forge and the Flame.* New York: The Macmillan Company, 1972.

Lubrano, John and Jude, "American Popular Music 1795–1920," *AB Bookman's Weekly,* Dec. 9, 1985.

Manvell, Roger, and John Huntley. *The Technique of Film Music.* New York: Hastings House Publishers, 1967.

Marks, E. B. *They All Sang from Tony Pastor to Rudy Vallee.* New York: The Viking Press, 1934.

Mast, Gerald. *A Short History of the Movies.* New York: Pegasus, 1971.

McCarthy, Albert. *The Dance Band Era: The Dancing Decades from Ragtime to Swing 1910–1950.* Philadelphia: Chilton Book Co., 1971.

Meyer, Hazel. *The Gold in Tin Pan Alley.* New York: J.B. Lippincott Co., 1958.

Mordden, Ethan. *Better Foot Forward: The History of American Musical Theater.* New York: Grossman Publishers, 1976.

————. *Broadway Babies: The People Who Made the American Musical.* New York: Oxford University Press, 1983.

Niles, John Jacob. *Singing Soldiers.* New York: Charles Scribner's Sons, 1927. Reissued by Singing Tree Press, Detroit, Mich., 1968.

Nite, Norm N. *Rock On.* Vol. 3, *The Illustrated Encyclopedia of Rock 'n Roll, The Video Revolution.* New York: Harper & Row Publishers, 1985.

Photoplay Treasury. Edited by Barbara Gilman. New York: Crown Publishers, 1972.

Priest, Daniel B. *American Sheet Music*

with Prices: A Guide to Collecting Sheet Music from 1775–1975.* Des Moines, Iowa: Wallace-Homestead Book Co., 1978.

Rachel, Frank R., and Sylvia G. L. Dannett. *Down Memory Lane: Arthur Murray's Picture Story of Social Dancing.* New York: Greenberg Publishers, 1954.

Rosen, David M. *Protest Songs in America.* Westlake Village, Calif.: Aware Press, 1972.

Rublowsky, John. *Music in America.* New York: Crowell-Collier Press, 1967.

Sampson, Henry T. *Blacks in Blackface: A Sourcebook on Early Black Musical Shows.* Metuchen, N.J.: Scarecrow Press, 1980.

Scott, John Anthony. *The Ballad of America: The History of the United States in Song and Story.* Carbondale: Southern Illinois University Press, 1983.

Shestack, Melvin. *The Country Music Encyclopedia.* New York: Thomas Y. Crowell Co., 1974.

Show Songs From the Black Crook to the Red Mill. Edited by Stanley Appelbaum. New York: Dover Publications, 1974.

Silber, Irwin. *Songs America Voted By.* Harrisburg, Pa.: Stackpole Books, 1971.

Silverman, Jerry. *The Liberated Woman's Songbook.* New York: The Macmillan Co., 1971.

Singing Soldiers: A History of the Civil War in Song. Selections and historical commentary by Paul Glass, musical arrangements by Louis C. Singer. New York: Grosset & Dunlap, 1968.

Songs of the 1950's. Introduction by Stanley Green. Winona, Minn.: Hal Leonard Publishing Corp.

Songs of the 1960's. Introduction by Stanley Green. Winona, Minn.: Hal Leonard Publishing Corp.

Spaeth, Sigmund. *A History of Popular Music in America.* New York: Random House, 1962.

Stearns, Marshall and Jean. *Jazz Dance: The Story of American Vernacular Dance.* New York: The Macmillan Co., 1968.

Stern, Lee Edward. *The Movie Musical.* New York: Pyramid Publications, 1974.

"Studying U.S. History Through Song." *Social Education,* Journal of the National Council for the Social

Studies, October 1985.

Thomas, Tony. *Music for the Movies.* New York: A. S. Barnes & Co., 1973.

A Treasury of Stephen Foster. Foreword by Deems Taylor, historical notes by John Tasker Howard, arrangements by Ray Lev and Dorothy Berliner Commins. New York: Random House, 1946.

Up from the Pedestal: Selected Writings in the History of American Feminism. New York: Quadrangle, 1968.

Westin, Helen. *Introducing the Song Sheet: A Collector's Guide With Current Price List.* New York: Thomas Nelson, 1976.

Whitcomb, Ian. *After the Ball: Pop Music from Rag to Rock.* New York: Simon & Schuster, 1972.

————. *Tin Pan Alley.* New York: Paddington Press, 1975.

Wilder, Alec. *American Popular Song: The Great Innovators 1900–1950.* New York: Oxford University Press, 1972.

Wilk, Max. *Memory Lane: The Golden Age of American Popular Music 1890–1925.* New York: Ballantine Books, 1973.

Winstock, Lewis. *Songs & Music of the Redcoats: A History of the British Army 1642–1902.* Harrisburg, Penn.: Stackpole Books, 1970.

Witmark, Isidore and Isaac Goldberg. *From Ragtime to Swingtime: The Story of the House of Witmark.* New York: Lee Furman, 1939.

"The Little Village Church-Yard near the Sea." This rare E. T. Paull cover, executed by Rosenthal, is the only known existing copy (1898). *Collection of Wayland Bunnell*

Acknowledgments

During the course of researching and writing this book, we were fortunate enough to encounter numerous individuals whose time, assistance, and generosity helped to make the project not only more complete but also more personally rewarding. Our sincere appreciation is extended, therefore, to everyone connected with the book.

In particular, we should like to express our thanks to the staffs of the Library of Congress; the New-York Historical Society; the Library and Museum of the Performing Arts at Lincoln Center; New Jersey public libraries in the towns of Bloomfield, Maywood, Hackensack, and West New York; ASCAP; and BMI.

Larry Zimmerman, Kurt Stein, Bob Greenberg, and Danny Crew, collectors par excellence, deserve an extra-special note of gratitude for their enthusiasm, sharing of expertise and resources, and generous permission to reproduce rare covers from their collections. Special thanks to Wayland Bunnell, the premier authority on E. T. Paull, for sharing with us not only his rare collection of Paull covers but also his singular expertise, without which the chapter and illustrations on E. T. Paull could not have been so complete.

Our appreciation to Dr. Deane L. Root, Curator of the Stephen Foster Memorial at the University of Pittsburgh, and Harriet Culver of Culver Pictures for illustrations; Mario Conti at Charles K. Harris Music Publishing Co., and Solomon Goodman for their efforts on our behalf; Ruth Phair and Gail Muller for locating music; and Roch Pulaski for the loan of music subsequently incorporated into the illustrations for this book.

Our gratitude and affection to Ellen Sheetz for the loan of her mother Nina's collection of 1930s and 1940s movie music; Dottie Harris at Collector Books for her support and belief in this project; Pat Cleveland, editor of Sheet Music Exchange, for her enthusiastic assistance with questions and research; Nancy Hancock for allowing us access to her master's thesis and, thereby, new insights into the early American women's movement; and Dr. Sally Roesch Wagner for generously sharing original documents on abolition and woman suffrage.

At Crown, thanks to Deborah Kerner, Mark McCauslin, and Milton Wackerow.

Lynn would like to personally thank her husband, Jeff, for his unflagging support and his willingness to donate weekends and evenings for this project, and her children, Jennifer and Michael, for their love and for listening to first drafts uncomplainingly. Special thanks and love to her parents, Ralph and Roberta Shallenberger, who filled her young life with music and literature and who have always been an unfailing source of encouragement and positive thinking, and to Jim, who always expected perfection but happily accepted less.

Carol would like to personally thank Elsie Reinholdt, Grace and Elwood Davis, Robert and Janet Davis, and Judith and James Knoblauch for their wonderful gifts of sheet music to her collection. She would also like to express special gratitude to her husband, Richard, for his constant encouragement and understanding as well as to her daughter, Daria, for her patience and companionship during the writing of this book. And she would like to particularly thank her parents, Dorothy and A. Robert Knobloch, for their valuable and ongoing support as well as for having provided the opportunity to pursue musical studies over many years that helped to lay the groundwork for this and countless other rewarding endeavors.

Last, but not least, we would both like to give special thanks to our agent, Susan P. Urstadt, and our editor, Ann Cahn, for believing in us and in *I Hear America Singing*.

Permissions

Authors' Note: The following items have been reproduced with permission of their owners as stated below. We have carefully researched and obtained these permissions in writing. Any error or omission therein is unintentional and any and all copyrights are the sole property of their rightful and legal owners.

Grateful acknowledgment is given to the following sources to reproduce the covers of songs listed below:

Chappell/Intersong Music Group—USA
"Now's the Time to Fall in Love" by Al Sherman and Al Lewis, copyright 1931 by Desylva, Brown & Henderson, Inc. Copyright renewed and assigned to Chappell & Co., Inc. International copyright secured. All rights reserved. Used by permission. "Follow Thru" by Lew Brown, Ray Henderson, and B.G. Desylva, copyright 1928 by Desylva, Brown & Henderson, Inc. Copyright renewed and assigned to Stephen Ballentine Music Publishing Co., Ray Henderson Music, and Chappell & Co., Inc. International copyright secured. All rights reserved. Used by permission. "Stay as Sweet as You Are" by Mack Gordon and Harry Revel, copyright 1934 by Chappell & Co., Inc. Copyright renewed. International copyright secured. All rights reserved. Used by permission. "For You, For Me, For Evermore" by George and Ira Gershwin, copyright 1946 by Chappell & Co.,

tional copyright secured. Used by permission. "At the Moving Picture Ball" by Howard Johnson and Joseph H. Santly, copyright 1920, 1948 by Leo Feist Inc. Rights assigned to SBK Catalogue Partnership. All rights reserved, controlled, and administered by SBK Feist Catalog Inc. International copyright secured. Used by permission. "Where Do We Go from Here" by Howard Johnson and Percy Wenrich, copyright 1917, 1945 by Leo Feist Inc. Rights assigned to SBK Catalogue Partnership. All rights reserved, controlled, and administered by SBK Feist Catalog Inc. International copyright secured. Used by permission. "(Hi-Ho-Lack-a-Day) What Have We Got to Lose" by Gus Kahn, Charlotte Kent, and Louis Alter, copyright 1933, copyright © renewed 1961 by Metro-Goldwyn-Mayer Corporation. Rights assigned to SBK Catalogue Partnership. All rights controlled, administered, and reserved by SBK Robbins Catalog Inc. International copyright secured. Used by permission. "A Hubba-Hubba-Hubba (Dig You Later)" by Harold Adamson and Jimmy McHugh, copyright 1945, copyright © renewed 1973 by Twentieth Century Music Corporation. Rights assigned to SBK Catalogue Partnership. All rights controlled, administered, and reserved by SBK Robbins Catalog Inc. International copyright secured. Used by permission. "Goodnight My Love" by Mack Gordon and Harry Revel, copyright 1936, copyright © renewed 1964 by Robbins Music Corporation. Rights assigned to SBK Catalogue Partnership. All rights controlled, administered, and reserved by SBK Robbins Catalog Inc. International copyright secured. Used by permission. "Would You" by Arthur Freed and Nacio Herb Brown, copyright 1936, copyright © renewed 1964 by Metro-Goldwyn-Mayer Corporation. Rights assigned to SBK Catalogue Partnership. All rights controlled, administered, and reserved by SBK Robbins Catalog Inc. International copyright secured. Used by permission. "Chant of the Jungle" by Arthur Freed and Nacio Herb Brown, copyright 1929, copyright © renewed 1957 by Metro-Goldwyn-Mayer Corporation. Rights assigned to SBK Catalogue Partnership. All rights controlled, administered, and reserved

by SBK Robbins Catalog Inc. International copyright secured. Used by permission.

Shapiro, Bernstein & Co., Inc.
"Rose of Washington Square," copyright 1920 by Shapiro, Bernstein & Co., Inc. All rights reserved. Used by permission. "Lookout Mountain," copyright 1917 by Shapiro, Bernstein & Co., Inc. All rights reserved. Used by permission. "Broken Blossoms," copyright 1919 by Shapiro, Bernstein & Co., Inc. All rights reserved. Used by permission. "The Beast of Berlin," copyright 1918 by Shapiro, Bernstein & Co., Inc. All rights reserved. Used by permission.

Shawnee Press, Inc.
"Charlie Chaplin Walk" by Roy Barton. All rights reserved. Used by permission. "Woman Forever" by E.T. Paull. All rights reserved. Used by permission.

Warner Bros. Music
"I'll Do It All Over Again" by A. Seymour Brown and Albert Gumble, copyright 1914 by Warner Bros. Inc. Copyright renewed. All rights reserved. Used by permission. "Hiawatha's Melody of Love" by George W. Meyer, Artie Mehlinger, and Alfred Bryan. Copyright 1920 by Warner Bros. Inc. Copyright renewed. All rights reserved. Used by permission. "Canadian Capers" by Gus Chandler, Bert White, Henry Cohen, and Earl Burnett, copyright 1921 by Warner Bros. Inc. Copyright renewed. All rights reserved. Used by permission. "Rock Me in the Cradle of Love" by J. Luebrie Hill, copyright 1914 by Warner Bros. Inc. Copyright renewed. All rights reserved. Used by permission. "The Japanese Sandman" by Richard Whiting and Raymond B. Egan, copyright 1920 by Warner Bros. Inc. Copyright renewed. All rights reserved. Used by permission. "I'm Forever Blowing Bubbles" by John William Kellette and Jaan Kenbrovin, copyright 1919 by Warner Bros. Inc. Copyright renewed. All rights reserved. Used by permission. "One Kiss" by Sigmund Romberg, Frank Mandel, Oscar Hammerstein II, copyright 1928 by Warner Bros. Inc. Copyright renewed. All rights reserved. Used by permission. "Limehouse Blues" by Douglas Furber and Philip Braham, copyright 1922 by

Warner Bros. Inc. Copyright renewed. All rights reserved. Used by permission. "My Rambler Rose" by Gene Buck, Victor Herbert, Louis A. Hirsch, and Dave Stamper, copyright 1922 by Warner Bros. Inc. Copyright renewed. All rights reserved. Used by permission. "Swanee" by Irving Caesar and George Gershwin, copyright 1919 by WB Music Corp. and Irving Caesar Music Corp. Copyright renewed. All rights reserved. Used by permission. "Smilin' Through" by Arthur A. Penn, copyright 1919 by Warner Bros. Inc. Copyright renewed. All rights reserved. Used by permission. "You're a Grand Old Flag" by George M. Cohan, copyright © renewed 1964 by Warner Bros. Inc. All rights reserved. Used by permission. "I'm a Believer" by Neil Diamond, copyright © 1966 by Colgems-EMI Music Inc. and Stonebridge Music. All rights reserved. Used by permission. "Diary" by David Gates, copyright © 1972 by Colgems-EMI Music Inc. All rights reserved. Used by permission.

Youmans Group
"Keeping Myself for You," copyright 1929 by Ceciley Youmans Collins and Vincent Youmans III. All rights reserved. Used by permission.

Grateful acknowledgment is also given to the following sources to reprint the material listed below:

Warner Bros. Music
Lyrics from "Halleluja, I'm a Bum" by Richard Rodgers and Lorenz Hart, copyright 1932 by Warner Bros. Inc. Copyright renewed. All rights reserved. Used by permission.

St. Martin's Press, Inc.
Quotations from *Scott Joplin and the Ragtime Era*, copyright © 1975, 1976 by Peter Gammond. All rights reserved. Used by permission.

The Bettmann Archive
Photograph of Vernon and Irene Castle. All rights reserved. Used by permission.

Culver Pictures Inc.
Photographs of Tin Pan Alley and Taft Theater. All rights reserved. Used by permission.

Foster Hall Collection of the Stephen Foster Memorial, University of Pittsburgh

Index